Fearless Learners

Six Simple Steps to a Student-Led Classroom

Christy Sutton and Kristin Westberry

For Maddox, Reed, Carson, Jackson, and Anna—

be fearless

Acknowledgements

To our students – *thank you for being innovators, dreamers, questioners, and world-changers. You continue to teach and inspire us more than you will ever know.*

To my family – *thank you for always encouraging me to find the humor, the good, and the possibilities. Thank you for loving me from calm to chaos and inspiring me each and every day. I love you more than words could ever express!* – ***Christy***

To my family – *you fill my life with laughter, adventure, challenge, truth, love, and more grace than I will ever deserve. Your faith in me never ceases, and my desire to make you proud only grows stronger. Thank you for the foundation of love and support that gives me the strength, courage and freedom to pursue my dreams. I love you all so much!* – ***Kristin***

Foreword

The deepest waters are the darkest, coldest, loneliest, and scariest, in contrast to shallow pools where warm water teems with life. Such is my comparison to those teachers who bravely venture into the abyss. To dive deep in one's profession requires courage and commitment...and a few lifelines.

As a principal, a leader of my organization, I see myself as one lifeline for those teachers who are brave enough to look at the research, trust their instincts, reach out to other teachers for support, and hone their instructional practice for the benefit of the students they serve.

What the teachers in this book do seems like common sense to me now...but it is not as commonplace as one might expect. Many in leadership positions speak about building better classrooms. We envision the teachers we want for our students: ones who will engage students...connect with them; ones who will inspire learning and know their impact on learning. We talk about this with other leaders and build professional development around fostering these qualities in our schools through the work of our talented teachers. But when it comes to seeing it in action, all too often we still find that we are falling short. Some of our students are not progressing at the levels we always hope for— but we can change this. We can engage our students and help them drive their own learning forward.

What happens when you open this conversation up to innovative teachers? What happens when you get out of their way and let them follow their instincts—when you let them fail and grow, and when you encourage them to learn from their students? You help them foster fearless learners. My hope is that we can continue to guide teachers like these through this powerful and promising process. This book will help both teachers and leaders alike through a truly transformational reform of our classrooms.

Sutton and Westberry captured me with their passion and moved me with their progress. They inspired me with the words of their students—not their own, but words grown from their nurturing and through their actions. They went where others would not. They persevered when others ridiculed. They shared their ideas, challenged mine, and pushed me into a better version of leadership. My hope is that they push you too.

Emily Harrison
Principal

Fearless Learners Contents

Step 1: *Start*—31

It all begins with a single decision: to start. Make the commitment to transform your classroom. Amazing things await!

Step 2: *Design*—79

This section will help you look at the current design of your classroom and will provide instruction and guidance for adapting it to meet the needs of a student-led environment. It is surprising what a few small changes can do to improve student engagement and bring back the joy of teaching.

Step 3: *Let Go*—125

Release control to gain it. Trust in your students. Give them choices and leadership roles in their learning—the sky is the limit!

Step 4: *Connect*—138

You are not an island. You have support. Connect with parents, students, teachers, and administrators, and stay active in your professional media groups (Twitter, etc.). Staying connected is key for *you* in the student-led environment.

Step 5: *Fail*—146

It happens, and it can be beautiful if you allow it to be. Embrace it instead of fearing it; from failure bloom growth and wisdom. You must jump in and be prepared (and even excited) to fail. Remember, you already have wonderful connections to help you through.

Step 6: *Celebrate*—162

You are fearless. Your students are fearless. Shout it from the rooftops. Celebrate! You (and they) deserve it.

Professional Learning Community (PLC) Guide—173

Your fearless group's six-week, interactive discussion guide. You'll meet, discuss, and journal together as you transform your classrooms.

Introduction

Student-led classroom? Does the mere thought leave you anxious? After all, students cannot possibly lead their learning. Certainly, that is the teacher's responsibility: we went to college; we attended approximately 132,000 hours of professional development; and we give up any semblance of a social life for ten months out of the year to do what we do.

Students are children. It just isn't possible…and even if it is, how can my evaluator click all those boxes if I am not standing in front of the class teaching? Each of these thoughts centered on the importance of the teacher, but what role was the student truly playing in the classroom? Changing the idea of teaching from teacher-centered to student-centered was the mind shift from which the student-led approach was born.

As teachers, we were amazed at the contrasting attitudes of our students, as some were more than willing to learn, while others did the minimum required to get through the class. We began to seek a true understanding of the difference in these two types of students. We tended to attribute these characteristics to capability, motivation, and support received, but as we observed our classrooms, we also discovered another trait, which showed up over and over again—fear. Our students who were innovators and leaders were fearless. They did not shy away from failure or opportunity. They jumped into the unknown with an unstoppable willingness. We thought of our own lives and how it felt to be fearless. It became the main goal of our classrooms—to create these fearless learners. From this idea, the student-led classroom truly began to take form.

How would you define student-led learning?

_____

_____

_____

_____

_____

_____

To us, the student-led classroom is centered on the individual; it is one that gives students empowerment to move at their own paces and take leadership roles in their learning. A growth mind-set is encouraged and modeled in a student-led environment. If we were to define a student-led classroom, it would be something along the lines of a classroom that recognizes, encourages, and celebrates the individuality of each student. In a student-led environment, the students take leadership roles in their learning by setting goals, developing their passions, and working at a pace that best meets their individual needs. This may not match perfectly with the definition you created, but it more than likely shares some of the same characteristics. On this journey, you should expect your definition to change as you adjust, learn, and grow with the student-led model.

In our student-led classrooms, students are taking ownership of their educational process. They are setting goals and understanding how to meet those goals. They each have a voice. Often, people confuse student-led learning with students being in charge of classroom management and teaching lessons. Nothing could be further from the truth. As you read this book, you will see the impact this approach has on each individual student. You will be able to implement these ideas in your own classroom and connect with other educators who have the same passion for teaching that you do. You will be supported and inspired and will act as an inspiration to others. In six short weeks, you will create a classroom that is engaging, motivating, and innovative.

We often hear the phrase "I didn't have anything *close* to a student-led classroom, and I turned out fine." Is fine good enough for our kids?

Maya Angelou said, "Do the best you can until you know better. Then when you know better, do better." We now know we can inspire a generation of critical thinkers, problem solvers, leaders, and lifelong learners. As educators, we can work together to make that the new normal. How could we possibly walk away from that?

We believe in the student-led classroom because we are living it. We know how it brought back the joy of teaching and how excited we are to come to school each day to learn alongside our students. We no longer see disengaged students whom we know we are not reaching. Our students love learning, and that will always be our biggest accomplishment.

This is not to say that everything has run perfectly since we started this approach. We often fail and have to re-create the wheel. We have had to defend the student-led approach from others who do not quite understand it (yet). However, there is never a day where either of us wants to go back to standing in front of the class lecturing to students. We do not miss depending on the textbook to teach the material or pushing students through the curriculum all at the same pace, no matter their actual level of understanding. We love what we do, and this book is intended to share the process that reignited that love. We want education to be meaningful for students, and we hope educators will regain their passion for teaching.

Christy's Journey

My journey to a student-led classroom cannot be defined in a moment. It was more of a series of events I will call an *educational awakening*. I think of this as happening in steps, over a period of several years.

I began teaching very shortly after having my first son. I am now the mom of three boys. Due to this, my teaching philosophies have been highly influenced by my being a parent. I always thought about what type of environment I wanted my children educated in. I began to consider my children's own classrooms – to think about how much their teachers could have missed out on. My boys were funny, capable, and highly intelligent in different areas. They also struggled with certain topics, but for different reasons. I wanted their teachers to know that, and some of them did. However, I clearly remember my oldest son being in a situation in elementary school where that was not the case. His teacher lectured throughout the day, and the students sat and listened. My son began to lose confidence and dread school. It broke my heart that he was overlooked and unnoticed.

Then I began to pay attention. I remember one day I was shopping and came across one of those Classroom Rules signs. It was adorably decorated, and I was sure others just like it were displayed in thousands of classrooms. At first glance, I might have even picked it up for my own classroom. Then I read it—"Listen to the teacher, sit quietly, raise your hand, pay attention." A little archaic, right? Where was the "Think creatively, be curious, take ownership, lead your learning" sign? I looked at my then-two-year-old. *He was curious*. He ran around amazed by the world. He loved to be read to and would bring books by the dozens to me begging for more information. He went outside and marveled at the world— amazing, vast, interesting…He loved learning.

I cried that night realizing that one day he might sit in a classroom and lose that. He would be told what to learn and how to learn it. He would have to be still and be quiet, raise his hand, pay attention, and listen to the teacher.

We all enter the classroom bright-eyed and ready to change the world. I mean, I have watched *Lean on Me*, *Freedom Writers*, and *Dangerous Minds*. I was going to do that! Well, reality sets in quickly in teaching. I had paperwork, testing, and data to work on first.

So, I began to slowly chip away at this idea of a building strong relationships with my students while also giving them a voice in the learning process. I talked to my students. *That* was eye-opening. When I asked them questions about their learning, there were two types of responses. Some knew exactly what they were struggling with—they just had not been asked. They could articulate it and even understood why they struggled in some areas. Others had no idea and were very uncomfortable talking about their learning. Oddly, this occurred more with my high-achieving students. They wanted to please me. They could pass any test I gave them, but when I asked them about what they wanted to learn about or areas they needed to work on, they were not sure of the "right" answer. I knew I had some work to do to meet the needs of both of these types of students. I began conferencing with my students more and giving them choices during center time. I knew I had a long road in front of me, but I could already see what an exciting journey it was going to be.

After moving to a new county a few years after beginning my teaching career, I was asked to coach an Odyssey of the Mind (OM) team. At the time, I had no idea what OM was or what coaching the team would entail. For those who are not familiar with OM, it is a club of sorts for students; it deals with problem solving, critical thinking, and teamwork. In the years since my first introduction to OM, I have become quite familiar with it, but that first year when I was asked to coach, I shrugged my shoulders and said, "Sure." I mean, after all, how hard could it be?

Well, it is an incredible organization and opportunity for students. Not only do they learn to work together to solve problems, but they also get to put these ideas into presentations, which they take to competitions from local to world levels. Some of my son's greatest memories came from OM. However, there are certain rules that are important to adhere to—the first and most important of which is the idea of no outside assistance being allowed. Teams are completely student-led. Adults cannot give ideas, help create sets, complete paperwork, write scripts for performances—nothing. Everything that is used in the competition has to be created by the students.

This was not easy. Each time they had an idea that I knew would lead them in the wrong direction, I had to stay silent. The biggest challenge for me was during the actual performance. The other coach and I sat front row, excited to see our kids perform. They had a set, and it needed to be brought out in a certain order. They had practiced this dozens of times. Yet on performance day, they were rushing and excited and brought the set out in the wrong order. I just had to sit there. I wanted to stand up and warn them of their mistake, but there was nothing I could do. Throughout their entire performance, the set was falling apart. Then something happened. They laughed. They ad-libbed and talked about how it must be termites. They had worked months for this moment, and when it did not go as planned, they adjusted. Due to their positive attitudes and amazing problem-solving skills, they ended up scoring quite well that year. I thought about all those practices and how I had listened to ideas that I did not think would work…ideas that I would have shut down if I had been allowed to do so. But some of them *did* work. Some of them worked very well; some of them didn't. But when they didn't, the students kept going. They adjusted and moved forward. They had created something, and they were proud—even when it was not exactly what they had envisioned. It made me consider how often I had held my students back because I had not let them explore ideas I had not thought would work. I still had a lot to learn.

Even today, I still use the OM problem-solving activities in my classroom. I want my students to trust themselves, move on when something does not work, and laugh when their set falls down around them, knowing it can always be rebuilt.

During the same time that I worked with the OM team, I had heard about Genius Hour and wanted to start this with my class. A colleague introduced me to the book *Pure Genius* by Don Wettrick. I ordered the book and read it within a few days. Talk about life-changing! Finally, an educator writing to educators in a meaningful way. It made sense, I connected—I was hooked. Genius Hour, or *Innovation Time* as I call it, started shortly after that in my classroom. The kids chose areas they were interested in and then explored them. They loved it, and I loved it! A seed was planted, and I wanted to see just how far I could take it.

An example of how Innovation Time impacted my classroom happened shortly after I implemented it. A student I had in my class enjoyed programming. He often went on different websites and created video games. One day, he was working on this during Innovation Time, and I reminded him that he was not allowed to play video games on the computer. His response? "I am not playing them; I am creating them. Do you want me to teach you?"

I knew then that I had made a difference. His willingness to teach the teacher proved that he saw himself as valuable in the classroom. It also made it OK for someone other than me to be the expert in the room. I became his Innovation Project for the next few weeks, and he taught me about programming. Now, programming is not exactly my passion, but seeing this student excited and engaged in learning was amazing. He went from a quiet and reserved child to someone with leadership skills and the ability to teach others. Try evaluating *that* on a standardized test.

I began creating scales that my students used to maneuver through their learning—not ones that were just on my board in case of an impromptu evaluation. I let the students work at their own paces on the projects they chose, and they also created our classroom newsletter. I allowed them to fail—I allowed myself to fail—and that was my biggest success. I let them debate the answers and talk about their learning process. They had conversations I wish were common among adults. They became excited and engaged; I became excited and engaged! Every day, it seemed as though we learned alongside one another. The students gave me different perspectives, and I became a better teacher because of it.

The remainder of *Fearless Learners* talks about the setup and setbacks of the student-led classroom, so I won't go into too many specifics. I will say I am amazed by what my students were able to accomplish. I had to learn to trust them and believe they could accomplish more. The funny thing about that is, when I did, they did. I think you will find the same is true for your class.

Kristin's Journey

The first time I was introduced to the idea of a student-led classroom, it was through this quote, which was projected on the screen for us to read during a staff meeting:

If you leave work every day exhausted, your students may not be doing enough.

Boy…did that hit home.

The simple shift in thinking that quote evoked was so powerful. As I sat right there in my uncomfortable cafetorium seat, reading the quote and rereading it, it caused me to ask myself, "Wait—does my classroom model really glorify and ignite my students' love of learning through *actively engaging them to lead the way* in the learning process, or does my classroom glorify the arduous efforts of my own lesson plans through *the lessons, presentations and demonstrations I carefully prepare for my students*? I didn't like my answer to that question.

There were a few eye-opening events that led me to the powerful decision to switch to a student-led classroom. Probably the most dramatic and moving event of them all happened last year at a Botball Florida regional tournament. For the past five years, I have coached an after-school robotics team called Botball. The team designs and builds robots using building blocks and metal pieces; makes them mobile and intelligent with motors, sensors, and servos; and then programs them so that they can perform tasks autonomously. Let me just say that I'm not a "robot person"—like most people, I think they're cool, but they aren't my hobby. I don't build villages with building blocks around my house in my free time, and before Botball, I had never written even one line of code. During my first year of teaching, I was asked by a teacher with too much on his plate if I would take the team over for him. (Remember how we can't say no to anything that first year, and everyone in the school knows that?) I agreed to sponsor the team, much to the delight of my very crafty coworker, and I was terrified. I read, studied, and talked to others about the program until I at least understood the goal for the team during the competition, and then

I called my first informational meeting. The meeting day arrived, and fifty-one exuberant middle schoolers filed into my tiny classroom (maximum capacity twenty-five). As they tried to find seats, I watched and listened to them—giddy with excitement, talking to one another about various robotics kits they had at home and the cool contraptions they had built, and chatting about programming languages they had experience with. I remember feeling my blood pressure rising, knowing more unquestionably with each passing second that I—the omniscient teacher and leader of this team—was actually the least-experienced, most unintelligent person in the room.

I had two choices at that moment.

Choice #1—I could capitalize on my blood pressure/adrenaline spike and go into defensive mode. I could march to the front of the classroom, demand silence and order, and then force them to listen to the things I *did* know about the Botball program. I mean, I was the teacher/leader, right? I was supposed to be in charge and know more than those kids. I could fake it.

Choice #2—I could capitalize, instead, on the energy and enthusiasm of the students, let go of my need for control (gasp), take a back seat, and put them in charge of leading the team—channeling their collective passions and background knowledge and encouraging their ideas in sort of a support role.

So what choice would you have made? It seems so clear and obvious to me as I write this now—but in that moment, I did what the pre-transformation teacher, Kristin Westberry, thought she had to do. I flicked the classroom lights a few times until the students were all quiet; then I marched to the front of the classroom to awe the students with the tiny bit I knew about Botball...with an amazing (amazingly boring) PowerPoint I had made, mainly composed of competition dates and deadlines.

Over the next few years, the time I spent with my Botball teams became my favorite hours spent at school—some student leaders emerged as I got to know them better, I gave up more and more control, and the team really took off. We competed each year at a regional tournament against middle school and high school teams from all over the southeastern United States. In our fourth year, we won second place in the competition—and this was absolutely HUGE for us! During the elimination rounds of that particular competition, our middle school team of eleven- and twelve-year-old students beat high school team after high school team until the very last round of the competition. To earn that second-place trophy was such a great accomplishment! The parents, students, and I cheered like crazy through tears of joy.

But the event that led to the switch—the *student-led transformation*—wouldn't happen until my fifth year of Botball. See, I had learned over the years that there are so many things that have to happen behind the scenes for the robotics team to be successful, and I had gotten really good at doing them all.

First—a practice board had to be built. Botball provides detailed architectural drawings with precise measurements on how to construct this eight-foot-by-eight-foot practice table. It's complicated and detailed, requires cutting and assembling lots of pieces of PVC and couplings, and the board is different every year, so it's an annual task. I recruited the help of my brother-in-law, Jack, who is by nature a skilled carpenter, and by trade, an engineer. Over the years we had developed a system: I'd shop for all of the PVC and other supplies, and he would cut them all precisely and label them, and together we would assemble the giant practice board—usually on a weekend. Watching the students' faces as they observed our masterpiece each year was always a highlight of the season for us.

Next—Botball requires that the students document their progress over the season in a series of five documentation periods. Intensive rubrics are provided for the documentation submissions. In plain English—this meant that the team had to write five detailed, perfect scientific reports and submit them in specified formats according to various dates and deadlines set by the program. This documentation counted as one-third of our overall score at the regional tournament. It was important, so I wrote every single one of those reports myself. (Middle school students couldn't be trusted to write them perfectly, right?) I followed the rubrics and submitted each report on time—cheering along with the students as we received feedback and great grades on each of our submissions.

Now we arrive at the event that led me to the *switch*. A new school opened closer to my home during year five of Botball, and as fate would have it, my incredible principal was the one selected to open it! I followed her and started a Botball team at the new school. The new team had a great first year together. We prepared for the tournament and anticipated great performances from our robots. When we arrived at the tournament, I was immediately surrounded by my old school's team. It was so exciting to see them again! Some of them had even started up a team at their high school since they were now in 9th grade. After some hugs and catching up, the two lead students from my old team and I were talking, and one student, Vihaan, said something that I will never forget—something that continues even now to help me make powerful changes, both in my classroom and as a parent to my own children. He said, "Mrs. Westberry, after you left we learned *so* much! We had *no* idea how much *you* did. You did *everything*! This year has been so awesome, because we got to do all of it ourselves!"

His friend readily agreed, and they told me about everything they had "gotten" to do that year:

- They got to plan all of the fundraising themselves. (They'd had to raise over $2,000 to compete.)
- They got to struggle through reading the blueprints and architectural drawings for the year's practice board.
- They got to shop for all of the required, specific PVC pieces needed to build the board.
- They got to be resourceful and find a way to get all those pieces cut precisely.
- They got to assemble the practice board together.
- They got to write all of the scientific reports and submit them on time, and they got to celebrate their own feedback and grades on those reports.

And guess what. Their team—my old school—won first place overall in the competition, and my new school took second. As my former students rattled off all of the things they'd "gotten" to do that day, it dawned on me that by doing the heavy lifting for my students I had actually robbed them of what might have become some of the richest educational experiences they would have as preteens. I cried that afternoon and again that evening; I have replayed that conversation in my head a hundred times since. If I was strolling toward *the switch* before my conversation with those two boys that day, I was pedal to the metal from that point forward. I am a teacher, and I am responsible for developing skills in my students that will prepare them to passionately, confidently and relentlessly pursue their dreams beyond the classroom someday. That conversation marked the dreadful discovery that my students were missing out on amazing learning opportunities *because* of me, the one who was supposed to be in charge of *giving* them these opportunities. I decided that day that no current or future student of mine would miss another great learning moment because I was doing the learning for them.

Guidelines for This Six-Week Classroom Transformation

Here's what to expect:

We are imagining that you are part of a group of teachers, big or small, who are excited about the idea of a student-led classroom and want to try transforming your classrooms together. If you are on this journey solo (you maverick), that works too, but we encourage you to sign up for the Facebook group "Fearless Learners" so that we can help you connect with others who are going through the transformation in the same ways you are. In addition to reading and journaling your way through this book, we have provided a PLC Discussion Guide in the back of the book. The PLC Discussion Guide includes a reading plan and action steps which will lead you through the transformation of your classroom; it is also designed around the assumption that you will be involved in a weekly meeting time with a group of other teachers (either in person or online). We feel that the collaboration with others as you shift toward a student-led classroom is critical—that is why the online groups are there for you to join if you are trying this by yourself. Your results after transforming your classroom will be so great that you'll want to share them with others outside your classroom walls anyway, and meeting with your groups or sharing stories online will give you just that opportunity. Your stories and feedback will inspire us and other teachers across the world as we work together in our grassroots effort to improve education for our children.

Requirements for each participant

1. This *Fearless Learners* journal/book.

2. Membership in the "Fearless Learners" group on Facebook (just search and join!).

3. Thirty minutes of weekly PLC meeting time with a group of people who are on this journey with you in their own classrooms.

Fearless Learners will guide you through a six-week transformation. Most of the journaling, reading, and exercises will be completed individually, but we encourage your group to meet weekly to discuss and evaluate your progress. We've prepared discussion guides for your team's weekly meetings, although we won't be offended if you go off the beaten path and just relish the time set aside for some unscripted conversation. (After all, we are teachers, too.) We're proud to share the results of our personal classroom transformations anytime we have the opportunity and truly anticipate the same experiences for each of you.

Step 1: *Start*

We've learned lately that when we're passionate about something or when we feel we are truly being called in a certain direction, it's always rewarding when we push our fears aside and simply take action right away. Since you are reading this, we know that you feel called to change the learning landscape for your students. You have everything you need to make this powerful change in your classroom already—without spending a single dime for some special program, series, or kit. Our students don't have time to wait for funding for the latest glamorous program that claims to reach and teach all students perfectly. They don't have time to wait for the government to decide if this or that set of standards or systems of accountability for schools and teachers might just be the magic pill needed to cure education in our country. We need inspired, passionate, intelligent, and open-minded teachers like you to *get started* now, make some simple changes inside your classrooms today, and give our future the education it deserves.

Now is the time.

Just start.

Maybe some of you reading this right now are thinking, "In theory, all of this sounds great. In a perfect world, teachers would have classrooms filled with motivated students who would be eager to lead their own learning. But we don't live in a perfect world. This wouldn't work in my classroom. I don't teach the gifted population. I teach struggling learners. They need strict rules and guidelines or they'll do nothing."

Believe me; we have had the same exact thoughts and doubts. Simply placing more value on the possible benefits, pushing aside our doubts, and just *starting* has been all of the proof we've needed to see just how much time we wasted waiting to begin—wondering "What if...." The best advice we can offer to teachers interested in transforming their classrooms into personalized, student-led learning environments is...trust your instincts and begin now.

It's fun to spend time visualizing change, watching inspirational videos or reading case studies, wishing our classrooms and education in general could be this way or that. But inside our classroom walls, we continue to stand and lecture to disengaged students in the same ways we always have. True change comes from actually taking that first step.

Start.

Behind those five letters is a surge of faith…a true commitment to making a necessary change—one you believe in…a change you make for reasons that stem all the way back to when you knew you *had* to teach. Are you ready? Roll up your sleeves and mark this date down in your journal.

Transformation begins: _____

Congratulations—you're already miles ahead of most others, moving toward revolutionizing education one classroom at a time by making this simple commitment.

Even after we became completely sold on student-led, personalized learning and were committed to transforming our classrooms, it still took us too long to get started. We wasted a lot of time making excuses, worrying, and doubting. Looking back, we both wish that we'd had the courage to make that critical and liberating switch years ago. Hopefully our stories and this step-by-step guidebook will help settle your fears and set you up to get started faster than we did. Time is a precious gift, and even more precious is the time you spend molding and shaping the future through your students. There is no time like the present.

Let's get going!

Transforming your classroom into a student-led environment that creates fearless learners takes some work at the beginning. (You'll learn about this in the next chapter, "Design.") Now that you are ready to get started, our first question to you is this: Are you open to it?

Indicate where your answer falls on this spectrum:

|--|

  Not really   Yes, definitely

What thoughts went through your head to lead you to that answer?

_____

_____

_____

_____

If your answer fell nearer to the "Yes" side of the spectrum, this journal will provide you with the guidance and step-by-step support you'll need to make your transformation a reality. Welcome aboard! Using our stories, steps, and guidelines, you (and your like-minded, change-agent teacher friends) will not only make spectacular transformations for your students inside your classrooms, but you will also draw energy and motivation from one another as you share your own unique and personal experiences along the way.

If your answer fell nearer to the "not-so-much" side, why not try the journal anyway? There is no way we could remember or put to use every single thing we have read or heard about, but as we have moved through our lives, little pieces of everything have touched us and stuck at different times, molding and shaping us into the teachers we are today. During this journey through *Fearless Learners*, if you learn or discover just a couple of things that help you improve your craft or the learning environment you provide for the children you teach, it will have been worth it. We know, however, you and your students are in for something much better, much deeper—maybe even the educational awakening of a lifetime. It's just so simple and logical that you'll wonder, like we do sometimes, why you haven't always let the students lead their learning. Read on.

The reason we decided to present the student-led classroom to you as an interactive, transformational journal, rather than as a simple read-along guidebook for you to follow, is that it's tough to *not* take action this way. The journal is an invitation to participate *actively* in your own transformation rather than passively being fed information on how others have done it. (Do you see where we're going with this?) You can read thousands of books about flying airplanes and become somewhat of an expert on the textbook mechanics behind what's involved in flying a plane, but until you've truly put that knowledge into practice—many times—we're pretty sure no one would fly with you. It's safe and easy for us to enjoy the comfort of theory—reading about, learning about, and enjoying the *idea* of transformational classroom change is pleasant and even inspiring. But true transformation takes action, and it is our sincere desire that this journal makes you hop to it. Our future is waiting.

Note your thoughts and reactions so far:

_____

_____

_____

_____

Like most things in life, your attitude and expectations for the results of this transformation greatly affect the overall success you and your students will have with it. Henry Ford once said, "Whether you think you can or you think you can't, you are right." Place a check next to the positive outcomes you anticipate from changing up the traditional school model and personalizing learning with your students:

- ☐ more meaningful relationships with my students
- ☐ increased enthusiasm and engagement among students in my classroom
- ☐ decreased (or complete lack of) discipline/classroom-management issues
- ☐ higher grades/assessment scores
- ☐ a comfortable, busy, and productive classroom environment
- ☐ students receiving immediate and personalized feedback on each and every assessment
- ☐ students discovering new strengths and abilities and proudly sharing them
- ☐ students who willingly move themselves beyond the county pacing guides or grade-level standards
- ☐ a buzz around the school – one created by your students - that your classroom is the place to be
- ☐ a completely peaceful, pleasant, and prepared feeling coming to work every day

☐ Strange looks from other teachers in your building who wonder why it is that you are always so happy and why the students going to and from your classroom seem to have the same attitude as you

Even if you didn't check all of the positive outcomes listed above, we will share that transforming your classroom to a student-led, personalized model will absolutely yield these results and much, much more. Believe—and let your transformation begin!

Consider for a moment something so basic that it's almost funny seeing it in print. Salman Khan, the creator of the innovative Khan Academy, says that the two foundational ideas that drove him to create the Khan Academy were: "lessons should be paced to the individual student's needs, not to some arbitrary calendar; and that basic concepts needed to be deeply understood if students {are} to succeed at mastering more advanced ones" (Khan 2012, 20). It seems so logical and simple to understand that since all individuals learn at varying paces, children should be taught at varying paces, and they should deeply master concepts before moving onto new ones. Right? But isn't that what we do in education today? We busily push each group of children along through lessons, through the pacing guide, toward the test date, etc., shaking our heads and doubting our teaching methods or "the system," as there always seem to be those students who don't master the content or just can't keep up with the pace. Khan concludes, "Even a one-to-one {student-teacher} ratio is not ideal if the teacher feels forced to march the student along at a state-mandated pace, regardless of how well the concepts are understood. When that rather arbitrary "snapshot" moment comes along—when it's time to wrap up the module, give the exam, and move on—there will still likely be some students who haven't quite figured things out. They could probably figure things out *eventually*—but that's exactly the problem. The standard classroom model doesn't really allow for eventual understanding. The class—of whatever size—has moved on." (Khan 2012, 21).

The transformation of the current classroom model is logical and necessary, and it needs to happen for every student in every classroom. We know you are probably wondering exactly how to create the student-led environment; you may even be looking for the exact steps, like the recipe for making banana pudding or the instruction manual with numbered steps for setting the clock in your car. But just like the steps for setting the clock in your car would most likely be different than the steps to set the one in mine, the steps we took to create our student-led classrooms probably look a little different than the ones you'll take, because we're different people—we teach different subjects and students, and we work in different environments. We've put together a one-size-fits-all, very general list of steps for you in the next couple of pages, but our hope is that you will view this guidebook more like a compass than a roadmap. The six simple steps we promised and provide to you in the chapters ahead are really just phases of your transition. Each unique teacher, with each unique group of students, will do things uniquely and differently. Sharing stories from your own transformations and the discoveries you make during the process will help us all learn best practices as we continue to refine our student-led environments. So here it is—the one-size-fits-all series of steps for the transformation from a traditional classroom to a student-led classroom:

1. **Discuss** the student-led classroom concept/model with your students and get their feedback.
2. Use the student feedback from the first step to **brainstorm** and decide how the student-led model will work/look in your classroom.
3. **Choose a unit of study in one subject area** to begin with. Using the standards you're teaching from, design an assessment for that unit. Design a pre-assessment as well...one that students can use to prove to themselves

that they're "assessment-ready." In the middle school math class, a student will take the pre-assessment and review the results immediately and individually with the teacher. That student may then request the graded assessment from the teacher if she feels she has mastered the content, or she may choose to practice or review something further before she's truly assessment-ready.

4. Now, think about the **learning activities and resources** you'd like the children to experience and actively participate in as they explore these standards and move toward becoming assessment-ready. How can you make these resources available to the students to use at their own pace? We've used menus, checklists, roadmaps, etc. to organize these resources and guide the students as they lead their learning. Here's a quick example of a student-led roadmap, including teacher check-ins (formative assessments) along the way to encourage frequent communication and feedback:

- ☐ In the paper file *and* on Edmodo, you'll find the **Module 16 Spiral Math Review**. Score 80 percent or above for a ticket. (Check your answers with me).
- ☐ Label a page in your math or growth notebook, "Mean, Median, and Mode." Watch this video for review, using earbuds. In your notes, write down everything Mr. Khan writes on the video. Show me your notes. Teacher initials: _____
- ☐ Textbook pages 451 and 452, explore Activity 2. Answer questions A–D and the Reflect Question #4 on page 452. Check answers with me.

- ☐ Khan Practice: <u>Mean, Median and Mode</u>.
- ☐ MAD mini-lesson with me. Teacher initials:

  _____

- ☐ <u>MAD Khan Practice:</u> Get five correct in a row and earn a ticket. (Show me five green checks, or send me a screen shot if you're working at home.)
- ☐ Whole-class lesson on constructing box plots. Just check this box when complete.
- ☐ <u>Practice Box and Whisker Plots</u>. Get three in a row correct.

We keep resources organized around the room in a way that is easy for the children to locate, access, and share together; these correspond to each unit of study. You'll learn more about creating student-led units in the "Design" chapter.

5. Target the unique **areas needing physical or procedural change in your classroom** to make the new model functional, taking the student feedback into consideration.

4. **Make the necessary physical and procedural changes** in your classroom.

5. **Teach your students the new classroom processes**, emphasizing the areas that were designed using their feedback, so that there is a confident and seamless transition with student buy-in and ownership.

6. **Roll it out!**

Think briefly about timing. As you can see, you'll need some time behind the scenes to plan and set things up. First, you'll need to introduce the idea to your students through a classroom discussion and brainstorming session (Discussion Guide on page 61). Then, you'll need to plan your first student-led units. For us, it took a few weeks of completely dedicating our planning time to preparing for the switch before rolling it out. In our world, this translates to one complete, eight-hour workday devoted to planning out those first units. The remaining units can then be planned out in your allotted planning time as you go. Remember, the student-led units you are creating are essentially becoming your new lesson plans. You'll spend some time making physical changes to the structure and organization of your classroom to accommodate new procedures. You'll also need to build in time to teach and practice the new classroom procedures and processes with your students. In middle school, introducing and practicing new procedures took roughly one ninety-minute block. In elementary grades, two weeks were spent implementing the new model. There were many talks about expectations, how to read and use the scales to understand their goals, and how we were not competing to be first—our goal is to master the standards.

Before we get too far into your classroom transformation, though, we thought it would be beneficial to give you a glimpse of what a day in the life of our student-led classrooms looks like. That is depicted below. As you move into the design phase of your transformation, more ideas from our classrooms, including many from the secondary classroom, will help you create a mental picture of how the model might work in your own student-led classroom.

A Day in the Life of an Elementary

Student-led Classroom

My students enter the classroom beginning at 8:00 a.m. However, school does not officially start for another thirty minutes. During this time at our school, teachers are supposed to "hold and monitor" the children until school officially begins. This used to be somewhat wasted time. I would encourage students to read or work on tasks they had not completed, but they were often off task, and I was either meeting with someone or greeting students at the door. It did not exactly start off our day in the best way. So today, as the students enter, I think of how much the student-led classroom has changed this morning routine. In our afternoon meeting yesterday, each student had planned out his or her schedule for today. If they typically arrive closer to 8:00, they begin their schedule at that time. For my students who arrive at 8:30, they begin their schedule then. No one misses anything or just does busywork while we wait.

Today, I stand at the door and greet happy, excited students. They come in, take out their planners, and review their daily schedules that they created. They also have their "must-do" lists, which are all the things they have to accomplish this week. (This would include cold reads, vocabulary quizzes, projects, etc.) They usually take a few minutes to look over everything and reacquaint themselves with their plans for today. Students do not have assigned seats, so they just choose one to act as a home base for them that day. They take out any notes or paperwork and let me know if there is anything I need to be aware of before our 9:00 a.m. meeting. Then, they get to work. Students have access to the assessments and assignments for the week, so some pick these up and work quietly at their desks. Others are on the computers working on a project or practicing a skill. Some are working in groups. Each morning, today included, I listen to those conversations, and each day I am amazed. They have a sense of pride and responsibility in their learning, and they take that very seriously. Today, three boys sit together and talk about fractions. They have decided to create a game for the class to practice equivalent fractions. They are talking about exactly what needs to be covered in that standard and have decided to look online to get ideas for lessons and games that meet the requirements.

Students continue to come into the classroom, check their planners, and get to work. I have one student who has walked in and is feeling pretty social today. He is taking his time with his backpack and talking to the students around him. I overhear him ask the group of boys if he can work with them, and they respond by saying yes, but only if math is on his schedule for this time. It is not, and shortly he begins working on "Main Idea" (the ELA skill that he has scheduled from 8:15 to 9:00). Another student just walked to my desk and picked up her reading assessment that she needed to retake. She had scheduled the retake for that morning after she had made sure to give herself enough time to meet with me earlier in the week to review the skill.

At 9:00 a.m., everyone goes to their desks, and we have our morning meeting. These usually last about twenty minutes for us now, although they were thirty minutes at the beginning of the year. During this time, I collect paperwork and go over anything students need to be aware of for the day. Then I randomly select a student to lead the morning discussion. Today, it is Lillian, one of my shy girls. She jumps up, goes to the front of the room, and begins to ask questions. She asks students where they are in the learning, what their goals are, and anything specific they are currently working on. I beam with pride, because a few months ago, she never would have been comfortable in front of the room. This discussion branches off to a couple of others (as it typically does). Students offer to help each other or ask to work on a project with someone else. Lillian is in charge of time though, so at our twenty-minute mark, she reminds everyone to work hard and make himself or herself proud.

At 9:20 a.m., I begin meeting with my scheduled groups. Today, I have three groups scheduled before our 10:30 a.m. resource time. I am briefly meeting with two students who have an idea for an Innovation project they want to ask me about. We brainstorm ideas until they have a general idea of how they want to structure it, and we plan to meet again at the end of the week. My next group meeting is math related. I asked this group of students to meet with me to strengthen their skills with comparing fractions. They each struggled with a mini-assessment and needed extra support. We meet for thirty minutes, and then they work together on an activity. My third meeting is to work with two students for math enrichment. These two boys are always looking to be challenged. They are part of our class's math enrichment group that we have scheduled once a week. However, they had requested to meet with me again, because they are excited about learning new math skills. I know better than to ever turn down these meetings, because that motivation can easily be stifled. We talk about using the distributive property when completing three-digit multiplication problems. These students have mastered our current standards, and encouraging them to think at a deeper level is exciting.

At resource time, the students are lined up before I finish groups. I am always finishing right at the last minute. (Sometimes groups run long. I was lucky today.) When they come back, they have about twenty minutes before lunch. Eight students had scheduled computer time now, but we only have four computers, so they have to work together to come up with a compromise. I do not schedule groups during this time because my morning groups usually go over time. Since they did not today, I spend this time walking around and making sure I talk to each of the students I have not yet met with today. I end up sitting with a literature club group. They are reading *Chocolate Fever* and are discussing the readings they assigned for one another in their last meeting. I sit back and just listen to their conversations. They have grown in their ability to be listeners and leaders, and again, I cannot help but be incredibly proud of them.

After lunch, I meet with our coding group. They are working on Scratch.mit.edu and are taking turns coding a project. They are happily laughing as one person makes a cat talk and another makes it dance. The coding group always gets a lot of attention because they are always having fun. At times I have to remind them to "Keep it down" so they will not disturb other students. I learn something new each time I meet with this group. Today, it is about repeating a step. I am a member of the group and participate with them.

After coding, I take time to walk around and help where needed. I have four students currently testing. One is taking a cold read, one a math assessment, and two others, science assessments. I talk with each student today, even if it is only briefly. I stop the class to celebrate with one student who has been hard at work practicing multiplication fluency. I read over another student's essay on Harriet Tubman and schedule a time to meet with her tomorrow. Then I help settle a disagreement between two students who are having a hard time compromising while working on building a roller coaster to study energy in science. We have spent quite a bit of time discussing our classroom community. Although these disagreements do occur, they are often easily resolved because of our discussions about respecting one another and being kind.

At 1:30, we come together for thirty minutes for our afternoon meeting. Again, I randomly select a student to lead the discussion. This afternoon, it is Mark, who loves being in front of the class. He is somewhat of the class clown, and he struts to the front of the room, which makes everyone laugh. He then asks students about the day— their successes, failures, advice, etc. These conversations are so important, because they encourage students to begin thinking about the next day's schedule. From 1:45 to 2:00 p.m., students write their schedules for tomorrow. When writing their schedules, they consider where they are in their learning and what they need to accomplish to meet their goals. Anything they did not finish today can go on tomorrow's schedule. Students talk during this time to schedule their groups for tomorrow as well.

The day ends with recess. At dismissal, I stand at the door and say good-bye to each student. The student-led classroom has definitely changed what the classroom looks like. I still work every second of every day, but I am no longer exhausted, defeated, or overwhelmed. I feel as though I am truly teaching, because I have the opportunity to reach each and every student. I end my day as I began it…smiling.

Grab a calendar. What are your thoughts on timing? If you're lucky enough to be reading this over the summer or during an extended holiday break, planning your rollout will be a piece of cake! Rolling it out during the school year is more difficult but absolutely doable. We both managed rollouts during the school year. So wherever you are, and considering all unique and potential variables (upcoming holidays or breaks, standardized testing, the amount and distribution of your personal planning time, family or personal commitments, etc.), create a rough schedule for your own rollout below:

Week #	Task	Target Date
1	Classroom Discussion and Initial Student Survey with Exit Slip (pages 61 and 62).	
2	Classroom Redesign Student Survey (page 76)	
3	Design/Planning Time	
4	Continue Design and Planning	
5	Train Students on New Procedures and Practices	
6	Roll Out the Student-Led Classroom	

As you can see, there are some things you'll need to do to prepare your students (and actually, yourself) for the change before jumping in.

First—let your students think through and discover for themselves how a student-led, personalized classroom could positively impact the way they learn in the classroom. We will lead you through this process in the next few pages.

We began our own transformations by simply pitching the idea to our students in casual classroom discussions, like a family talking about possibly planning a vacation over dinner one night. We started the discussions by asking our students, "Have you ever been working on an assignment or a test you felt you were unprepared for, struggling to answer even the first questions? That's an awful feeling, right? Have you ever struggled on a test or an assignment, but you felt that the kids around you seemed to think it was no big deal—like everyone was getting it but you?" Like we did, you'll have a group of students who can identify closely with these feelings. How about you—as an adult; have you had similar experiences?

Have *you ever felt that you were* behind "the middle"? *Think about a recent training, PLC, or staff meeting, and jot down how you felt during that time here:*

_____

_____

_____

Next we asked the students, "Now how about this...have you ever had to sit through a lesson on something you were already really familiar with? Have you ever started a unit or been asked to do a lot of work on things that were too easy for you—that you already knew how to do? Have you ever had to sit around patiently listening to other students asking question after question in a whole-group setting while you felt like you could just go ahead and take the test and move on?" You'll have some hands, just like we did, shoot up in agreement with this sentiment too.

How about this scenario? Have you been there, either professionally or as a student? Jot some specific notes related to that memory below:

_____

_____

All of us have been both places at various times in our lives—we are all different, and learning certain things is easier for some people than it is for others because of this basic fact. Does that mean that not every student can master *all* of the content—that different types of individuals just may never be able to understand parts of the content? No. It just means that, for some students, it may take more time or some creative, alternative learning methods for them to truly and deeply understand things that don't come as naturally to them. The student-led classroom provides opportunities to reach every single student, right where he or she is.

In the student-led classroom, teachers are finally free to spend individual time with individual students and with small groups of students. As teachers, we know that's where the magic is. That's where we're able to use our personal knowledge of each child—his unique learning style, his interests, his strengths—to tailor our conversational lessons to him for maximum impact. In individual or small-group settings like this, lessons are conversational (two-way). The children feel confident asking questions or clarifying/summarizing what they've learned to make sure they're on track. These frequent, personalized discussions we have in our student-led classrooms consistently lead us to powerful discoveries. We unearth gaps in student knowledge and learning that sometimes prove to be the culprits behind that dreaded feeling of "just not getting it." Who knows how long those gaps might remain gaping and widening if we just continued group teaching and group testing? Students might miss a few questions here and there in their individual gap areas, but still we would march on through the pacing guide, marking down the 70 percents or 80 percents in the gradebook, calling that *mastery* and moving on. How much "moving on" would it take for a confident, capable student to eventually have skipped over so many gaps in understanding that he or she begins to struggle, then loses confidence and becomes disengaged? Isn't every single child worth it?

Take Jacob, for example. He is a bright, capable, A/B student in my standard sixth-grade math class. Jacob is admired by his peers as a leader in the classroom—he always makes the highest grades, and he always offers the right answers during classroom discussions. When I am busy with students and others need help, they always gather around Jacob's desk for assistance. He is confident in his abilities and so am I. Working through the decimals unit one day in the student-led model, though, he hit a road-block. Suddenly there was something he didn't know how to do. I was working with a small group of students across the room that day, but I could easily see Jacob's frustration from where I sat. Since he was the only one in the classroom who had advanced to the particular concept he was working on (dividing decimals), there was no one in the room he could work with. I called across the room that I'd be over to help him soon, and with his head resting in one hand, he waved me away with the other, saying, "I got it, thanks." While I admired his perseverance and his "I got this" attitude, I made a mental note to visit him when I finished with my group. A few minutes later I walked over to his desk to check on him, ready to help him out of whatever was dragging him down. When he noticed me coming over, he said, "Look at this, Mrs. Westberry! When you're dividing, you can keep adding zeroes in the dividend so that you get a *precise* decimal answer in the quotient. The zeroes don't change the value of the dividend at all, but they help you keep dividing. I always thought you had to just write the first remainder up as the last digit in the quotient. *That's* why I kept missing these and couldn't move on. Now I'm getting them all right! I'm almost ready to level up. I'll probably make a one hundred on the pretest now." I'm pretty sure I got real tears in my eyes at that moment—and moments like these in our classrooms continue to stop us in our tracks and make us wonder why it took us so long to make the switch. The skill he had just learned was a fifth-grade skill—one he needed to perform the sixth-grade skill he was currently practicing. It was a gap. Not only did Jacob know exactly what skill he needed to master this completely, but he understood the standard on which he was about to be tested *and* he independently sought out a way to learn that unique skill on his own (he used Khan Academy). He proved to himself (through practice) that he had mastered it; he articulated *why* his discovery was so important (it helped him generate more "precise" answers—an amazingly mature discovery for a sixth-grader) and told *me* that he was almost assessment-ready. All of this is wonderful, right? But for me, the real beauty of this moment was that Jacob had found and filled a little gap in his understanding, thanks to the student-led model. In the traditional school model, there's a good chance Jacob would never have discovered that gap; he would've taken the test, missed the two or three questions related to precisely dividing decimals, and moved on with his eighty-five or so. He (and I) would've moved right on, glazing over the fact that a little gap in understanding existed because the test grade was OK. That gap would have continued to widen over the years until it became a real cavity. Now, maybe Jacob would have read the feedback I had written on his test about adding zeros—but maybe not. Maybe, in the traditional school model, if I had built in time to review each student's individual mistakes with him or her following the test, perhaps the gap would have been noticed and filled that way. That would be great, right? But what teacher in the traditional model truly has time to personally review every mistake with every student following every assessment? The class and pacing guide must move on. That type of one-on-one guidance is only possible in the student-led model, and it is critically important.

What are your thoughts on students working at their own pace? What are your concerns?

_____

_____

_____

_____

_____

So why do we continue to teach a topic for a week or so, test on the topic, maybe offer a retest for students who don't show mastery (but rarely do we offer any real re-teaching prior to the retest), and then just move on? Discuss this with your students.

Ask your students if they would be excited to know that they could take some extra time to learn things that were tough for them to understand. Explain that a student-led classroom expects every student to learn and master the standards, but it allows them to do so at varying, individual paces. Ask them in your next breath if they'd enjoy being able to skip over sections of classwork on topics they'd already proven mastery in.

Explain to your students that in a student-led classroom, students would take tests only when they were assessment-ready. This means achieving true mastery of the material. Assessment-ready is not "I have studied and I can pass the test." It is "I understand the material well enough that if I was given an assessment at any time, I would get a high score." This would look different and happen at different times for each student or group of students in the classroom. Not every student in the classroom will be working on the exact same thing at the same time. Students will be very independent—leading their learning—and this responsibility will require the development of a great deal of maturity and perseverance.

Look back at the dates you recorded on page 52. By the classroom discussion date you listed, before you begin planning your rollout, you should have this whole-class discussion with your students, asking the questions we just covered. In summary, lead a discussion with your class asking the following questions:

Classroom Discussion Guide

1. Have you ever felt unprepared for an assessment—like everyone was "getting it" but you?
2. Have you ever had to sit through a lesson or complete work on a topic you already knew?
3. Do you think it is OK to let certain students get poor grades on tests and just move on, even if they haven't fully learned things?
4. Would you like to have the freedom to take a little more time to learn concepts that are tougher for you?
5. Would you like to be able to skip over classwork or assignments if you can prove you already know how to do them?

As your students leave your classroom on Discussion Day, provide them with this exit slip to collect their anonymous, honest thoughts on the idea of the switch. (You'll find printable/editable copies of this exit slip, designed for multiple grade levels, on our Facebook page)

Exit Slip

1. On a scale of 1 to 5, how much would you like to switch our classroom to the student-led model?

|--|

1   2   3   4   5

No way!   Neutral   Let's start
It'll never work.   tomorrow!

2. Write a sentence or two about why you answered number one the way you did.

_____

_____

_____

_____

Once you have collected, read, and reviewed all of the exit slips, jot down some observations from your students' responses that you'll share with your PLC group during your week two meeting:

_____

_____

_____

_____

As a side note, you will be surveying your students several times throughout your transition. We are providing survey documents to you via our Facebook page, but please feel free to incorporate the surveys into your own plans in ways that work best for you. We've collected survey responses electronically, on paper, and even with simple hand-raising. The key here is that you are about to make an important change in your students' classroom, and your students need to fully understand the reasons for the change, as well as to be a part of the transformation.

Tally your responses to question #1 on the Exit Slip, and average your responses. Write the average here:

_____

Now read the comments on any exit slip rated two or below. You will need to address any negative responses with the class, as you'll want complete buy-in to really make this transformation successful in your classroom. If students have fears or hesitations, talking through them may even help you as you develop your unique classroom design in the next chapter.

Record your thoughts after your classroom discussions and after collecting some student feedback via the anonymous survey. Your thoughts will help guide the week two PLC discussion:

_____

_____

_____

_____

It's time now to think about your classroom set-up and design. Before you can begin your classroom transformation, you're going to have to determine what changes need to be made in your current model/system. Let's target some specific areas for change, together with input from your students.

This part is both tricky *and* wonderful to write to you about, since it must be so uniquely *you*. No two designs in the student-led classroom are going to be alike, but each will be perfect in its own way.

We'll give you an idea of how we began. We began by picturing a happily humming, blissfully creative, and engaging student-led environment, where learning was visible all around us. Will your new classroom always feel that way? Maybe…but probably not. Imagining perfection, though, can help as you begin to mentally construct a uniquely functioning student-led model in your classroom.

As I thought about my own classroom in this way, I looked around and noticed things I'd have to change right away. I noticed the three giant dry erase boards in the back of the classroom, one labeled for each of my preps (standard sixth-grade math, advanced sixth-grade math, and algebra 1 honors). Under each heading was the learning goal listed for the day, which all of the students (in theory) would be mastering together by the end of that class period. Also listed was a unit scale for each prep and specific homework assignments. Well, with children leading their own learning and mastering the standards at varying paces, how could just one learning goal apply to all of them? The boards would need revision. Research and our own experience have proven that children perform better with a driving (or essential) question, learning goal/target, or objective. How could we still provide the students with the learning goals when they're all learning different things? Or better yet—how could we have the students define their *own* individual or group-learning objectives for the day?

Another thing I imagined as I pictured my perfect, student-led classroom was that there was plenty of celebrating going on as students accomplished their goals. As teachers, we love to see students delight in their accomplishments. It's easy to offer praise and give specific, positive feedback on student-offered answers or while passing back graded papers in a whole-group setting, but how would they share successes with one another in a student-led environment? In our school, we have a list of statements for student success that the students recite each morning. One of them is, "I celebrate my success!" I thought back to a time long ago when I had been a preteen gymnast. The girls at my gym all wanted to be great—we loved Bela Karolyi and Mary Lou Retton—but we weren't all on exactly the same level. Much like the premise of this book, we naturally progressed at varying paces. But we were a family, and we encouraged and cheered one another on through our individual journeys to be the best gymnasts we could be. In our gym, there was a simple bell we would ring each time we mastered a new skill. Ringing that bell was a big deal—any time the bell was heard ringing in our gym, we would all stop in our tracks and cheer for the girl who was ringing it. It meant hours of hard work, sweat, tears, guts, and belief/faith had finally paid off, and the girl ringing the bell had successfully completed the skill enough times to prove to herself she had "gotten it." My new, if not somewhat still ideal, student-led classroom was going to have to have a built-in system of celebration.

A question did linger, however, even as I imagined that perfect classroom. It hung over me; my mind kept returning to it, and I knew I'd need to address it appropriately as well. The question was—without structured guidelines, rigid test dates, consequences for not completing assignments on time, etc., how would I be sure that 100 percent of my students were staying motivated? (In fairness, although this is a very valid question—one we hear often from teachers concerned about making the switch—it is a question that is even harder to answer in the traditional model.) Sure, the majority of students would be eager to lead their learning—this concept would be exciting and even ideal for them. *But*—what about the student who claimed that he or she needed a super slow pace or way too much extra time to master certain grade-level standards? What system of checks and balances would need to be set in place for students who lacked the intrinsic motivation to lead their learning? (See "Fail" chapter for more detail on this topic.)

So spend a few minutes picturing students leading their learning in your classroom—considering all of the variables that make your classroom unique to you, your content, and your students.

What does it look and feel like?

Describe it here:

_____

_____

_____

_____

_____

_____

List several systems, practices, or procedures that might need to change once your classroom is student-led. Remember, the goal here is to give your students a voice. These changes do not have to be drastic. *What can you do in order to give each student more of a leadership role in his/her learning within your classroom?*

1.

2.

3.

4.

5.

Now list some ideas you have for tweaking or adjusting the items you just listed during your classroom transformation:

1.

2.

3.

4.

5.

Now for the fun part. Let's get your students mixed into the redesigning process. For us, this was a critical step in the process, and truly, it was the best part! The creative suggestions from our students blew our practical, mundane ideas out of the water. Their input transformed our classrooms into incredibly engaging student-led environments that were alive with both learning and camaraderie—so please, *please* don't skip the critical step of involving even the tiniest of stakeholders in the transformations of their own classrooms.

Look back at the things you listed on pages 69 and 70. Using the items or areas you listed, shape them into survey questions for your students.

For example, consider again the giant white boards in the back of my classroom. Each board contained specific learning goals that were updated daily as the herd progressed, all together at the same time (in theory), through the content. I wouldn't need specific goals listed for the entire class any longer with the new model. My survey question for my students became, "When we switch to the student-led model, students will be learning different lessons at different times. How will each of you know what you should be learning each day? How will you keep track of it *and* know what you'll be learning next? Also, since you'll all be learning at varying paces, we can erase those white boards in the back of the room. What could we use them for in our new classroom?"

My students' responses helped me create my "new" room. Before I surveyed the kids, my original thought was that we would keep the progress of each student confidential; I thought that publicizing the students' progress might embarrass the students working at a slower pace. The results of the survey, however, showed unanimous support for displaying student progress publicly in the classroom for all to see.

So, we developed a visual tracking system using ribbons and clothespins as seen below:

In my class, the curriculum is divided into units, and each unit is represented with one of the colored tags you see above. The ribbons represent each of my different classes. Students use teacher and student co-created roadmaps/scales to guide them through the learning activities for each unit. The students and teachers work on creating these scales and roadmaps in order to increase understanding of what true mastery looks like. The learning activities vary for each unit, but some examples include scheduling individual or group mini-lessons with the teacher, completing practice on or offline, playing games, watching video tutorials, reading from the textbook, creating foldables, blogging or journaling exercises, designing study materials for the class to share, working together on projects, going on scavenger hunts—just to list a few. I try to widely vary the types of activities in order to reach and appeal to every type of unique learner I teach. Also included on the road maps are several formative assessments—"checkpoints" —so that students can check their understanding along the way. Some of these are self-assessed, while others require the students to check in with me. I build frequent teacher check-ins into the student roadmaps, mainly through mini-lessons and formative assessment checks, and these check-ins provide the wonderful conversations with students, where I spend roughly 90 percent of my day. These conversations happen with every student, multiple times per class period, and they provide personalized feedback for the students on their progress, as well as teaching or re-teaching opportunities if needed. Students document their learning activities in growth journals (individual student composition books they keep in the classroom). Once they feel they've mastered the content in a unit, they take a unit pretest. When they finish the pretest, we meet to evaluate together if the content has been mastered and if the student or group of students is ready for the unit assessment ("assessment-ready"). When each student finishes a unit assessment, it is reviewed and graded immediately, with a one-on-one conversation happening at the same time—instant, personalized feedback. Once they've successfully completed their unit assessments, they move their clothespins up to the next unit and grab the next unit roadmap. You don't have to use ribbons, roadmaps, or growth journals— like we said, the system you design needs to be unique to you and your students. Teachers we know have had success displaying student progress in countless ways, from using markers to complete simple charts on the wall, to representing each student as a laminated mountain climber, climbing a paper mountain of knowledge on the classroom wall. Find what works for you and your students, and share your design on our Facebook page!

Another question for my student survey was developed from my vision of having students cheering one another on as they accomplished their goals. My question became, "In our classroom, how will you stay motivated to keep learning? How will you celebrate your success?" It turns out that (second only to earning candy) the students really wanted recognition from their peers when they accomplished things. We decided to incorporate a bell, similar to one you'd ring to grab the attention of a store clerk at an empty desk. Now, each time a student moves his or her clothespin up to the next level, he or she also rings the bell. Everyone cheers each time someone rings the bell, and somehow we eventually added taking a victory lap around the classroom, complete with leaping over chairs and high-fiving random classmates in celebration. It will look different in every classroom, but celebrating success keeps the positive energy in our classroom at a level that's almost palpable.

Using your brainstormed lists from pages 69 and 70, create corresponding survey questions you'll use to gather feedback from your students. Get ready to feel *their enthusiasm in their responses!*

1.

2.

3.

4.

5.

Schedule about ten minutes this week to administer the
survey to your students and collect their responses.
*Read through your students' thoughts, searching for trends
or common themes in their responses. With a highlighter
(or digital highlighting tool), note and highlight the things
that seem to appear common across the student voices
and jot them here:*

_____

_____

_____

_____

_____

_____

Your students' thoughts, along with the thoughts from your PLC group's students, will help you discern best practices while designing your student-led classroom. Next steps— make some changes to your classroom and teach the students about them.

You know, Harry and Rosemary Wong gave us a classic idea in their *First Days of School* book—more effective teaching and learning really does occur when students and teachers are familiar with the processes and practices (routines and rituals) that are unique to each classroom. The foundation of their teaching is that "The teacher is responsible for organizing a well-managed classroom where students can learn in a task-oriented environment" (Wong 2009, 83). The student-led classroom is no different. Although you will be making substantial changes to the traditional school *model* in your classroom, the new processes and practices that accompany the student-led model will still need to be taught and practiced by all before effective learning can take place.

You've committed to this transformation. You've gotten your students excited about the new model. You have an idea of how the model works in a couple of different classrooms and have pictured what it will look like in yours. You, your students and your PLC group have thought about the changes you'll need to make along the way. In the next chapter, "Design," you will be actively and productively designing your new, student-led classroom.

Step 2: *Design*

Studies have identified a significant "skills gap" between what students are currently being taught and the skills employers are seeking in today's global economy. Our children must be better prepared than they are now to meet the future challenges of our ever-changing world. —Stephen Covey, The Leader in Me: How Schools and Parents around the World Are Inspiring Greatness, One Child at a Time.

Design—even the word itself is difficult to define. *Webster's Dictionary* says to design is: "to plan and make decisions about (something that is being built or created)" (*Merriam-Webster Online* 2016). Design is personal. It *is* about planning and making decisions. There is not a one-size-fits-all design plan that just works for the student-led classroom. One of the joys of teaching is decision-making. As teachers, we often forget we have the power of change. We are tied to legislative, administration, and parental decisions. We underestimate the value of our own decisions.

The current popular classroom design demands that students learn. We expect them to learn at a drastic pace. Students are reading by kindergarten, completing high school credits in middle school, and taking high-stakes tests from the moment they begin their school careers. We give them millions of pieces of information and then expect them to repeat it all back to us in the form of an assessment. Yes, we expect them to learn, but did we ever teach them *how* to learn? Did we ever teach them how to pursue their interests and develop their curiosity? Sir Ken Robinson (whom we could quote time and time again) gave a TED talk in which he asked if schools are killing creativity (Robinson 2006). If you haven't seen this presentation, please do. He raises a valid question. How are we defining and measuring the student's mastery of a given topic? Are we fostering a love of learning, of exploring, of problem-solving in real-life applications?

The National Association of Colleges and Employers recently completed a survey with a sample size of 260 employers asking what skills they look for when hiring (Forbes, 2014)

The ten skills employers seek, in order of importance, are

1. ability to work in a team;

2. ability to make decisions and solve problems;

3. ability to communicate verbally with people

4. ability to plan, organize, and prioritize work;

5. ability to obtain and process information;

6. ability to analyze quantitative data;

7. ability to assimilate and use technical knowledge related to the job;

8. ability to use computer software programs with proficiency;

9. ability to create and/or edit written reports; and

10. ability to sell and influence others.

Are you currently teaching these skills daily in your classroom? Remember, our students are future job applicants. We can honestly say that several years ago the answer in both of our classrooms was no. Our students were not learning to prioritize and make decisions. We completed all these tasks for them. We told them what they would learn and when they would learn it. We knew some students already had the skills necessary to move forward, and some had gaps in their learning that needed to be filled before they started a standard—but we did not know a better way. The student-led model truly develops these skills in every one of our students. We know that not only are they mastering the content but they are also practicing and cultivating the skills that their future employers will want.

If you could change three things about the current education system, what would they be?

1. _____

_____

_____

2. _____

_____

_____

3. _____

_____

_____

Now, take a second to look at those changes. Do they seem overwhelming? Impossible? Think of ways to relate them to your classroom. Here's an example—testing. We are not fans of state and district testing. We value the data and feedback testing provides; however, we are over-testing our students and often cannot view the test, so the data becomes less valuable. Yet the main reason we do not like testing is the stress it puts on the students. They look defeated or overwhelmed at the thought of these high-stakes tests. They rarely feel confident or prepared. The problem is, there is nothing we can do about these tests. They are required, and there is no magic wand to make them disappear. What we *can* do is look at what changes we can make inside our own classroom walls. The compromise? No whole-group testing. The students in a student-led classroom test when they are ready. They test when they have mastered the material—not because it is Tuesday at 1:00 p.m., and that is when we have decided everyone should have mastered the skill. It turns out that change has had a ripple effect. It has reduced retakes because students are no longer pushed through the material at a pace that doesn't fit them. Since students in the student-led classroom are used to feeling confident and prepared, state testing no longer bothers them. They even welcome the chance to take the test, because they *know* they have mastered the material. No longer are they defeated with low scores over and over throughout the school year because they were pushed through the material. Win-win, right?

Think of your teaching career. Do you remember your first observation? You most likely over-prepared for it. It may have gone very well, but it was not necessarily a true reflection of your everyday teaching. This same concept applies to our students. They know a test is coming, they study for it, and they do well…but it does not necessarily indicate a true or complete understanding of the topic. This is why students can receive a high grade on a test but not remember how to successfully complete those skills a month later. They never had a deeper understanding of the content. As you became more comfortable in your teaching, your observations began to be a more genuine reflection of your everyday classroom. Someone could walk in at any time and complete a positive observation. As students become more comfortable with a skill, you will be able to assess them at any point, and they will do well.

What three changes can you make inside your own classroom to make each student's educational journey more rewarding, giving them opportunities to practice the skills employers want?

1. _____

_____

_____

2. _____

_____

_____

3. _____

_____

_____

We have taught gifted, ESE, lowest 25 percent, and high-achievers in our classrooms. The student-led approach has worked with all of these student populations. Yet this model does look different in each class. You know your strengths as a teacher. You know your students. We have said many times, "Do what works." But we should be doing what works for the students—not just doing what is easiest or least controversial. What is the greatest benefit to the students, who depend on this educational system for their futures?

So far, you have completed a survey and had conversations with your students about their feelings toward a student-led model. You have looked at your classroom and discovered what adjustments need to be made in order to support a student-led environment. You have even thought of how you will visualize student progress and how students will be able to track their learning. Congratulations! You are well on your way to creating an environment that encourages fearless learning. As you continue to work through the design step, remember—design is personal. You will make adjustments in your design. If you are like us, you will make a lot of adjustments. It is a process...a journey.

Enjoy it.

Using the survey results you collected in the last section and the idea exchange from last week's PLC, make the physical transformations your classroom will need to facilitate the new student-led environment. *Note the changes you plan to make here, and check them off as you complete them.*

- ☐ _____
- ☐ _____
- ☐ _____
- ☐ _____
- ☐ _____
- ☐ _____
- ☐ _____

Along with physical changes in your classroom, your first few student-led units of learning will need to be designed.

We are not textbook dependent. We use scales to lead students through their learning. Scales are essentially the standards the students must master. They help our students track and assess their own learning. Students have access to these scales for each unit of learning during the school year. They keep them in their growth journals or notebooks and document their learning as they progress.

We co-construct the scales with our students. We use the standards given to us by our state, as well as our county's pacing guide, to develop the level 3 portion of the scale. Level 3 is "grade-level proficient," and it is the goal of each student to reach that level. We have a class conversation to decide what knowledge and learning make up levels 1 and 2. The students discuss what vocabulary they need help with or what concept that may need to know before reaching a level 3. Here is an example of a scale:

Name: _____

Scale:

Level 4:   CHARGE ON!

Level 3: I can:

_____consistently use the correct units of measurement when calculating area and perimeter.

_____ measure the area of a shape by counting the square units and/or using multiplication.

_____ understand the difference for calculating the perimeter and area of an object and know the appropriate calculation for each.

_____ solve word problems with real-world applications involving area and perimeter.

Level 2: I can:

_____ understand the vocabulary: area, perimeter, square units.

_____ calculate area when asked to do so.

_____ understand how to calculate perimeter when asked to do so.

Level 1:

_____ I am learning about perimeter but still need support calculating it.

_____ I am learning about area but still need support calculating it.

_____ I do not yet understand the difference in perimeter and area.

- Please date the scale after each checkpoint and get your teacher's signature

*Standards accessed from www.fldoe.org.

Here is another example of a scale. This one includes some sample problems students should be able to solve with confidence at varying levels of mastery. Some students like being able to quickly self-assess their learning needs by seeing how far up the scale they can confidently solve problems or answer questions:

Sample scale with self-assessing problems:

4	**Can you:** Create and solve scale problems using proportions?
3	**Can you:** If 1 of every 4 bikers at POA has a blue bike, how many blue bikes would a group of 256 POA bikers have? **Can you:** What's the better buy: $6.90 for 6 rolls of paper towels, or $13.68 for $12 rolls? What is the unit rate for each? **Can you:** Solve this proportion: $\dfrac{x}{27} = \dfrac{8}{18}$?
2	**Can you:** Write the ratio of (1) boys to girls, (2) girls to boys, (3) boys to total students and (4) girls to total students in our class? **Can you:** Write the ratios above in three different ways?
1	**Can you:** Define these words: ratio, rate, unit rate, equivalent ratio, proportion, ratio table, scaling, scale drawing?

Mastering the actual standard is considered a level 3 on the scale, and what the students need to know prior to mastering it is covered in levels one and two. The students typically determine level 4. We call that the "Charge On" level, because it goes with our school mascot, the Charger. Students need to know what it looks like when they have mastered the material, so having examples is a very good idea. They want to see what success looks like, and they need help visualizing this—especially when starting a new concept. We construct these scales with the students, but we base them on our county's curriculum pacing guides. It is important for the students to understand the standards and the wording, and for the scale to reflect where they are actually starting their learning, considering their previous knowledge and what they need to learn. We have included additional samples of our scales from both elementary and middle school on our Facebook page "Fearless Learners." These scales require you and your students to understand your state's learning standards. It is amazing how eye-opening it is when you truly take the time to research the standards for your grade level/subject.

How well do you feel you currently know the standards for your grade level/subject area(s)?

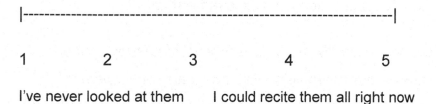

We once had to complete an activity with other grade-level teachers where we were given several standards, and we had to match them with their appropriate grade levels. It turned out to be very difficult. As teachers, we thought we knew what the expectations were, but none of the groups in our training matched even half of the standards correctly. We thought other grade levels were responsible for teaching material that was actually part of our grade level's curriculum. We did not have a clear understanding of what skills students entering our classrooms had mastered. We had such high expectations for our students, but we did not have a clear view of exactly what those expectations were. One of the problems we had was that our standards had changed a couple of times over the previous few years, and we had just not kept up. It was a good learning opportunity for us, and we began to see the importance of really knowing our standards—as well as those in the grade level below and above us. After all, in order to effectively help our students, we need to know where they came from and where they are going. This also helps us identify those gaps we discussed earlier.

Do you currently use scales in your classroom? After viewing our example scales, how can you implement scales in your own classroom, or what changes could you make to the scales you are currently using?

_____

_____

_____

_____

_____

_____

How do you plan for your students to track their progress?

_____

_____

_____

_____

_____

_____

One of the first things we did was that we committed to allowing students to move at their own pace. This means no whole-group testing. We wanted students to test when they had mastered the material. Some could test right away on a topic because of their prior knowledge. Some struggled with a concept and needed a few extra days to master that standard. Now, because students move at their own pace, we rarely have whole-group lessons. We teach students in small group settings or individually. We have come to know our students better this way. We can easily help them with individual struggles, because we are able to identify them more quickly. We also have stronger bonds with our students, which makes them (and us) much more motivated to learn. There is no child who "falls through the cracks."

Committing to students moving at their own pace will be the biggest leap in the student-led model. It is an interesting adjustment to organized and blissful chaos. It forces you to really get to know your students. We pictured students approaching us *when* they were assessment-ready and everyone getting As because they were so prepared. Well, one of the best things about children is their confidence, and you will find this to be both a positive and a negative in the student-led classroom. Some students will say they are ready to assess just to compete with other students. Others will never feel prepared even though they are more than capable. It is important that you lead students into the student-led approach instead of just throwing them in. They need to understand what the expectations are and how they will know when they are assessment-ready. You can start by doing a whole group pretest in the beginning of a unit of study, or even just before the actual test, to help gauge where the students are in their learning. You can also ask the students and start getting an understanding of how well they are able to determine where they are in their learning. We give checkpoints along the way so that the students can prove mastery of each individual skill before the assessment. This means no one can completely just skip a section, because we want to make sure each student at least reviews all elements of that unit before moving on. These checkpoints may be quick five-question mini-assessments, small-group meetings, essay questions, or any other way we can quickly check their understanding before they move on. This also stops students from spending a week working on a standard and then realizing that they really had not moved forward in their learning.

Following are several examples of student-led learning guides we have used. As you read through the list of learning activities, you'll notice a blend of personalized instruction time, collaborative problem-solving time in groups, individual practice time, formative assessments that are self- or teacher-assessed, and pre/post assessments at the conclusion of the unit. The students have paper copies of these for their notebooks, but they also have access to their scales and maps of learning activities online via Edmodo. This allows links to practice sites and videos to be live, and it allows students who are traveling, sick, or otherwise working from home to never skip a beat.

Module 16A—Statistics—Start Date:_____

Estimated time: three class periods plus assessment.

What are your five learning goals for this module?

16.1_____

16.2_____

16.3_____

16.4_____

16.5_____

Your Scale has been created. What's your level?

4	Can you: Conduct your own research, collect and analyze the data, calculate the measures of center, and choose/construct the most appropriate data display to share on our blog?
3	Can you: Create a dot plot, histogram and box plot for the data in the level 1 data set (12, 10, 7, 9, 10, 13).
2	Can you: Find **and interpret** the MAD (mean absolute deviation) of this set of average temperatures for cities in the southeastern US: 68, 71, 66, 70
1	Can you: Find the mean, median, mode and range of this data set? 12, 10, 7, 9, 11, 10, 13

Use the scale to assess yourself BEFORE learning: _____

Teacher checkpoint/initials: _____ How will we get there?

- ☐ In the paper file AND on Edmodo, you'll find the Module 16 Spiral Math Review. Score 80 percent or above for a ticket. (Check your answers with me.)
- ☐ Label a page in your math or growth notebook, "Mean, Median, and Mode." Watch video for review, using earbuds. In your notes, write down everything Mr. Khan writes on the video. Show me your notes. Teacher Initials: _____
- ☐ Textbook Pages 451 and 452, Explore Activity 2. Answer questions A–D and the Reflect Question #4 on page 452. Check answers with me. _____
- ☐ Khan Practice: Mean, Median and Mode. Show five green checks: _____
- ☐ MAD mini-lesson with me. Teacher initials: _____
- ☐ MAD Khan Practice. Get five correct in a row and earn a ticket. (Show me five green checks, or send me a screen shot if you're working at home.)
- ☐ Whole-class lesson on constructing box plots. Just check this box when complete.
- ☐ Practice Box and Whisker Plots. Get three in a row correct._____

- ☐ Do all problems on page 483 in the textbook. Check your answers with me.
- ☐ Pretest (paper in file or digital copy available via Edmodo)

Use the scale to assess yourself AFTER learning: _____

- ☐ Request assessment—Score _____ Where are we going next?

Student-led means that students will be at different places in their learning each day. We do get questions about how we manage it, and there are two answers to this. First, we teach the students how to understand where they are in their learning and give them a lot of responsibility in tracking their progress. Second, we talk to every student, every day. We meet often in small groups, but we also make time to walk around and check in with everyone daily. Building teacher checkpoints (formative assessments) into the students' learning activities fuels our continuous conversations and meetings with our students each minute of the school day. During these meetings we review assignments, projects, or formative assessments personally with the students—providing immediate and personalized feedback and re-teaching or filling gaps where necessary. We also set up conference sign-up sheets so students can always let us know if they need help. We can tell you our step count has increased drastically since starting this model! However, knowing where each student is in their learning is not difficult, because we have truly developed a relationship with each of them, like this one:

> There was a student named Jon in my class. I was already implementing the student-led approach, but I knew I still had so much to learn. This student opened my eyes to the possibilities of this design and why it is so critically important.

> That year, Jon was my biggest challenge. Now, when I hear people refer to challenges in their classes, it usually means that student is a behavior issue. He cannot sit still or she yells out. Well, those things are true of Jon, but that is not why he challenges me. He was my biggest challenge because I cannot keep up with him. He is my biggest challenge because the work I give him is not his biggest challenge. He always seems one step ahead. He once told me school bores him. Every time I feel like I am going to stump him, he comes to me five minutes later with a gleam in his eye and a completed project in his hand. He has become my mission.

> Today, he is making a building out of papier-mâché. A fellow teacher asked him why, and he told her all about the learning scale he was

creating for physical change, measurement, and data. The idea that he was just doing arts and crafts quickly exited her mind. Jon smiles all day. He may be ahead of the game, but he still plays every day. He finds ways to challenge himself, and every once in a while, I give him something that takes him hours. He eagerly works at it with an excitement and love of learning that makes everything I do worth it.

Now, there is another Jon out there. One labeled "gifted" who sits in a classroom that includes lectures about topics he already knows. He has learned to not listen. He has disengaged. That Jon is sitting on a 100 percent average because he knew all the answers to the tests, but he could have taken them on the first day of school and saved 180 days of his life. Or maybe he has a 70 percent average because he does not care much anymore. I think about that Jon a lot. I know his teacher knows he is smart, but does she know he is capable—capable of things like papier-mâché projects and writing learning scales and developing games for other students? Probably not. I wonder how many Jons I failed because I wanted to be the smartest one in the class.

Once I saw my students who were pleading to be challenged, I made some changes. By the way, we talk a lot about "underachievers" and how to reach them. I honestly feel that many people challenge their students by giving them more work. Look at it from their perspective. If you did a great job as a teacher and just ended up with more paperwork to complete, would you be motivated? I wouldn't. So I had this in mind when I decided to change things: more challenge but not more work. Not an easy problem/solution.

Remember when I mentioned my scales and how they lead my instruction? They are leveled 1–4 with a level 3 being the goal. Level 4 was meant to be the next step, and I wrote them out and told the kids to try to get there. That equaled more work—more of the same work, just harder. No one wanted to go to a level 4. Why would they? Then one day a group of teachers and I were discussing scales and how to co-construct them with students. We wanted students to be part of the process. They needed to be active participants in their learning. We started talking about level 4 and why the scale had to be a checklist. It turns out there was no reason. Someone had done that, and we had all followed suit without much consideration to the practicality of it. We created the idea of level 4 being student-created with a real life application for the learning goal. (Maybe you are making the papier-mâché connection now.) Amazing stuff! My kids would learn fractions from cooking or building, they would learn addition while shopping, angles playing soccer—the possibilities were endless. Finally, they would be able to see exactly how they could use these skills in their everyday lives. And the best part—it would all be student directed. The students loved it. They were eager to pass level 3 to pursue their interests and find ways to relate them to what we were learning in class. The Jons of the class were finally going to be appropriately and personally challenged.

I was asked recently what will happen to my students next year if they are not in a student-led classroom. That question does keep me up at night. I think my answer has to be that I don't get to decide that. I only have them this year, and this year alone. I can help them understand what capable people they are. I can encourage them to think, to question, and to fail over and over again in order to find success. I can watch them become fearless. I can know that loving learning will always be more important than a reading level, or an A, or any test. They are amazing individuals, and I do not want to miss knowing them. I have them for 180 days, and I will make the most of it. I hope they reflect on it and say they learned more than any skill or standard.

Do you have a Jon in your class? Don't define Jon by his giftedness. Define him as a student who is difficult to motivate, to reach. *How did you handle this?*

_____

_____

_____

_____

_____

_____

_____

In what ways would a student-led approach be beneficial to this student?

_____

_____

_____

_____

_____

_____

During our design processes, we also have to consider the students who are completely overwhelmed. They have not mastered level 1, yet we keep pushing them further and further along until they feel completely lost and begin to disconnect. We start labeling them and calling them underachievers. We begin to intervene with our processes and special curriculum when really all they needed was a few more days at level 1. What if they had been given more time? We talked previously about how a small problem can become a big gap over time. Think of the tooth cavity analogy. If left untreated, a cavity will continue to grow until it creates pain and becomes very difficult to repair. If caught early, the process to reverse the damage is much easier. Often, learning gaps with students go unnoticed for too long and become harder and harder to fill. The student-led model helps us make sure we are providing each student with appropriate and timely help for his or her individual needs.

One of the most important things to encourage in the student-led classroom is that failing and experiencing setbacks are really just opportunities to learn and grow. We studied successful people and how they faced failure over and over again in their lives, emphasizing that each failure always prefaced growth—and successful people have the grit and determination to dust themselves off and get back up stronger after setbacks. We talked about how we are different and that we move, learn, and grow at different paces. We stopped the competition. We promoted the idea that learning is individual but that we all needed one another in the process. This type of environment isn't created overnight, but make sure you address any issues (growth opportunities.) that arise right away. Eventually, you will have a supportive group that values the uniqueness of each member's educational journey. Each student should feel comfortable enough to be honest about his or her strengths and weaknesses in order to really meet his or her learning goals.

We have student-led environments where students are moving at their own paces with clear understandings of their learning goals. We have students helping us develop scales, using specific examples of how students would complete checkpoints to show mastery of each standard. We even have students completing assessments as they become individually ready for them.

What standard/subject will you be starting on?

_____

_____

Now what? What are they doing the entire class period/day without us standing there lecturing? Oddly, they are learning—*really* learning. We give them resources—books, games, online activities, and the ability to work in groups. They truly are engaged in ways we have not seen before. We had always had movement and group work, but we often found students were distracted and off-task during this time, or that one individual was doing most of the work while the others rode coattails. This is different. They have choice, voice, and leadership roles in their learning, and they take that responsibility very seriously. This is not to say that we do not have to redirect students, but the amount of that has lessened. At first, many students hesitated when given freedom. They had never had it before and were not sure *what* to do when they weren't being told exactly what they should be doing. When we allowed them to talk without a strict structure, we were blown away by their ability to problem-solve and critically think about topics. We have stopped interfering to make sure they have the correct answers, and we've started allowing failure to become a celebrated growth opportunity in the classroom. The incorrect answer has become an *opportunity* instead of an *X* on their papers. They take more risks. They listen to one another. They smile when they enter the classroom. We are onto something!

What resources do you need to prepare in order to make the first unit in your student-led classroom a success?

_____

_____

_____

How will you give students opportunities to collaborate, problem-solve, and think critically?

_____

_____

_____

We often say we want to teach like parents *and* CEOs. What qualities do we want our own children to have? What qualities do we want in an employee? Many of these overlap. (None of them are test-taking abilities, by the way.) We do not want them to grow up and be listeners. We want them to be innovators using their gifts and unique abilities.

We want them to solve problems and to be contributing group members, motivated life-long learners, and productive citizens in their communities.

Thinking like a parent and a CEO, what are three qualities you want your students to develop?

1. _____
2. _____
3. _____

Does your classroom currently help develop these qualities? If not, what changes could you make?

_____

_____

_____

_____

_____

_____

_____

A teacher was telling us about a county in our area where the curriculum is completely scripted. We also have experience in this type of curriculum. Everyone is doing the exact same thing at the same time. The teachers literally read from a book all day, and the students sit at their desks, lifting their pencils or answering questions when prompted. There is no sense of individuality, no sense of exploration or innovation. Imagine being a student in that environment. Teachers can hardly sit through a staff meeting and pay attention, but we expect our students to have that attention span for an entire day, day after day, at school? Here is the truth—drill and kill works. It works well—for test taking. Models that allow students to problem-solve and critically think work well for *life,* as well as for testing—but that is secondary.

Which makes more sense?

Write three or four sentences to describe what an optimal learning environment looks like (personally) to you.

_____

_____

_____

_____

_____

_____

Now, write three or four sentences depicting an optimal learning environment from your students' perspectives:

_____

_____

_____

_____

_____

_____

Did these match? If not, think of why. Maybe because of control? As teachers, we feel the need to be in control. We think having a quiet classroom with a group of students looking at us as we perfectly explain some theory is what we are supposed to do. But what we are actually supposed to do is to ignite a love of learning within our students. Our classrooms are loud, and there is a lot of movement. We move from student to student and have real, meaningful conversations with them. We know they are learning the requirements, but they are also, and more importantly, developing the qualities of leadership, critical thinking, collaboration, problem-solving, and independence. These are lessons they (along with their future families and employers) will value forever.

Is there anything holding you back from fully implementing the student-led classroom?

_____

_____

_____

Once we began developing our student-led classrooms, we wanted to give students more opportunities to showcase their new leadership skills. We had open communication with the parents of our students throughout the process, but they still had questions. This was especially true in elementary school. Parents questioned if students were ready to handle the responsibility. So we decided to have students complete student-led conferences with their parents/guardians. They scheduled time to sit down with their parents and led a conference with them. We developed a form to help guide the students through the process. Then we asked for feedback from the parents.

Here is the form used in elementary:

Student-Led Conference

Student Checklist

_____ Welcome your parents and thank them for taking the time to meet with you.

_____ Open your planner and show your parent your daily schedule.

_____ Explain our Student-Led Schedule and how you feel about it. (Be specific, use details.)

_____ Explain your current Innovation Project and tell your parents how they can help you.

_____ Explain your plan to meet your current goals in ELA and Math and how your parents can help you.

After your parents ask you their questions:

_____ Thank your parents for conferencing with you, and ask them how you can help them at home.

Remember: When speaking with your parents, you want to give specific feedback. Saying "I don't know" or "Good" is not specific.

Parents,

Thank you very much for participating in this student-led conference. Your child is very excited to share with you his or her progress in our class. I value your feedback and appreciate you taking the time to complete this form during your conference.

Questions for your child:

1. What does your child feel is his/her greatest accomplishment this year?

_____
_____

2. What is your child most proud of learning?

_____
_____

3. What are some areas your child needs to work on before entering the next grade level?

_____
_____

4. What are his/her long-term educational goals?

_____
_____

Questions for the parent:

1. Do you feel this conference was worthwhile?

_____

_____

2. What did you learn about our classroom environment or your child's learning goals?

_____

_____

3. What feedback would you give your child's teacher about the year overall?

_____

_____

Please rate this conference from one to five (five being extremely beneficial and one being not at all helpful).

|--|

1   2   3   4   5

In Middle School, the student-led parent conference guide looked like this:

Conference Leader's Guide

1. Greeting and Introduction

☐ Thank your parents for attending your conference.
☐ Introduce yourself as the conference leader.
☐ Ask your parents to write your name on their form as the conference leader.
☐ Ask your parents to write the names of everyone who is attending your conference (and give them time to write).

2. Growth Journal

- ☐ Explain what the growth journal is.
- ☐ Tell your parents how we use the growth journals in class.
- ☐ Explain why the growth journals are important.
- ☐ Ask your parents to rate their understanding of the growth journal and how it is used. Give them time to circle their rating.

3. Module Talk #1

- ☐ Choose any module you would like to talk to your parents about.
- ☐ Tell your parents the name and number of the module, and give them time to write it down.
- ☐ Turn to that module in your growth journal.
- ☐ Go through the road map with your parents, explaining the learning activities.
- ☐ Give your parents *details* about the activities as you talk.
- ☐ Ask your parents to rate their understanding of the road maps and how they work, and give them time to circle their rating.
- ☐ Tell your parents about a major problem you faced during this module. Show them an example in your growth journal. Then tell them how you solved your problem. Give them time to write this down.
- ☐ Choose the thing you learned in this module that you're *most* proud of. Tell your parents about it—maybe even show them how to do or solve something. Give them time to write this down.
- ☐

4. Module Talk #2

- ☐ Choose one more module you would like to tell your parents about.

- [ ] Tell your parents the name and number of the module, and give them time to write it down.
- [ ] Turn to that module in your growth journal.
- [ ] Go through the road map with your parents, explaining the activities.
- [ ] Give your parents *details* about the activities as you talk.
- [ ] Ask your parents to rate their understanding of the road map and how it worked in this module, and then give them time to circle their rating.
- [ ] Tell your parents about a major problem you faced during this module. Show them an example in your growth journal. Then tell them how you solved your problem. Give them time to write this down.
- [ ] Choose the thing you learned in this module that you're *most* proud of. Tell your parents about it—maybe even show them how to do or solve something. Give them time to write this down.

5. Mastery and Goals

- [ ] Tell your parents that you have used your growth journal to identify a couple of areas you need more practice on before the FSA.
- [ ] Tell your parents about the first practice area and show them this section in your growth journal. Tell them why you need more practice with this. Give them time to write it down.
- [ ] Tell your parents about the second area you need practice in. Tell them why you think you need practice with this. Give them time to write it down.
- [ ] Tell your parents a specific goal you would like to accomplish before the end of the school year in math. Ask them to write your goal down on their form.

6. Overall Conference Score

- [ ] Thank your parents for listening and participating today.

- ☐ Ask them if they have any questions for you or for your teacher.
- ☐ Answer any questions they have for you.
- ☐ Write down any questions your parents have for your teacher here. (Tell them your teacher will e-mail answers to them.)
- ☐ Ask your parents to rate your conference. Once they finish your rating sheet, collect it from them. You will be turning it in for a grade—so please put it in a safe place!
- ☐ Write the date you finished your conference here:

  _____

- ☐ Ask your parents to sign their name(s) here:

  _____

Sample middle school letter to parents regarding the student-led conference:

Hello Families!

Welcome to the parent conference you can attend right from your living room! This conference should take no more than fifteen minutes, so—choose a convenient time and a comfortable, quiet place to devote to your **conference leader**:

_____

Parents, please complete and return this conference record by Monday, April 4. You may also submit the record electronically via e-mail if desired.

1. Conference attendees (please list all family members who listen in):

_____
_____
_____
_____

During this conference, you will be recording things you learn from your student conference leader. Let's begin!

2. **Growth Journal**: Your conference leader will explain the purpose of the growth journal. Please rate your understanding below. (1—"I'm still not sure what the growth journal is or why it is used" and 5—"I totally understand how the growth journal documents my student's learning in math.")

1   2   3   4   5

3. **Module Talk 1**: Your conference leader has selected two Modules to talk you through. During both discussions, please record information below. Feel free to ask questions during the conference.

Module selected (number *and* title):

_____

My conference leader explained the road map and how he/she used it to navigate the module. (1—"What road map?" to 5—"I thoroughly understand the learning progression as described by my child and his/her roadmap.")

1   2   3   4   5

Describe one major problem your student faced during this module:

Describe the method(s) he/she used to solve the problem or get help:

During this module, my child was most proud of learning:

4. **Module Talk 2**:

Second module selected (number *and* title):

_____

My conference leader explained the road map and how he/she used it to navigate the module. (1—"What road map?" to 5—"I thoroughly understand the learning progression as described by my child and his/her roadmap.")

1   2   3   4   5

Describe one major problem your student faced during this module:

Describe the method(s) he/she used to solve the problem or get help:

During this module, my child was most proud of learning:

5. **Mastery and Goals**: Using his/her growth journal as evidence, your conference leader should show you a couple (2) of weak areas he or she needs practice with before the FSA.

Practice area #1: _____

Practice area #2: _____

Describe your **student's goals** for the remainder of the year in math:

6. **Rate the overall conference** (1 = waste of time to 5 = learned all about my student's learning in math and enjoyed it):

1   2   3   4   5

These forms are also included on our Facebook page, "Fearless Learners." The parents were impressed by their children's ability to speak about their learning. They were surprised that they were so articulate and motivated about their learning. We received valuable feedback from parents and used their suggestions as we continued to tweak the student-led model in our classrooms. The conferences also allowed the parents to recognize the amazing academic capabilities of their children. These conferences are something we complete twice a year because the feedback is incredibly valuable.

We wanted to continue to give the students more opportunity to control their education—to feel empowered and responsible in their learning. In both elementary and middle school classes, our students design a good portion of their daily schedules. Now this looks different in both types of classrooms. In elementary school, students write their own daily schedules. If you walk into the classroom at any given moment, some students are working on math and some on ELA or science or social studies. There are guidelines for this work. They must complete some requirements (this is called our "must-do list"), and they have to schedule an hour of math and ninety minutes of ELA every day. They love creating their own schedules, and as much as people said there was no way a third-grader could handle that responsibility, there is a classroom of third-graders that prove that theory wrong. They can easily say, "I am working on Main Idea in Informational Text, because this is an area I do not currently feel comfortable with." Goosebumps, right? In middle school, the students work at their own paces and therefore decide what they are working on each day. They effortlessly talk about their learning goals and the steps they are taking to reach them. That does not mean your students have to follow this approach. Do what works. If the idea of different subjects at the same time is too overwhelming, just concentrate on giving students choice within one subject.

Another great thing about this approach is the stress it removes from taking the day off or having someone unexpectedly pop into your classroom. The students have taken ownership, so there *is* no bad moment to come in or no lost day because you were sick.

Write your current thoughts on creating your student-led classroom:

_____

_____

_____

We make sure to know our students. As part of this process, we always give students the opportunity to explore their interests. This is their Innovation Time. They have built robots, created cookbooks, researched and collected items for nonprofit organizations, and the list goes on and on. They also author our classrooms' newsletters and our classroom blogs. These are their classrooms, and their voices should be heard. You can find examples of these newsletters and blogs on our Facebook page. We often receive parent e-mails about how their children have started or continued exploring their interests at home. Motivation and wonder in the classroom beautifully spills over into all aspects of life, as it should.

In elementary school, we have also developed several groups students can participate in during our day. So far, we have coding, drama/literature, and accelerated math. These began as teacher-led groups, but that only lasted for about a week. As the teacher, I attend all these meetings, but I end up learning more than teaching.

One day I was scheduled to be in the coding group, but I realized I had double-booked my agenda to meet with another student. I talked to the coding group and told them I would be late. I explained that another student needed help with a concept and that I needed to be there for her. It never occurred to any of us to cancel the group that day. The students in coding understood and completed the meeting on their own. In the group, I am a member. If I cannot make a meeting, I owe the group an explanation just like any other group member. However, my absence does not mean the group cannot continue. This is also true if there is a sub or if I am pulled out for a meeting. It is a wonderful feeling knowing that my classroom carries on in my absence exactly as it would in my presence.

How will you allow students in your class the time to explore their own interests/passions?

_____

_____

_____

We know this approach sounds idealistic. After all, it is why most people don't get past *Start*, right? The impossibility of it all? Yet we have classrooms full of students who talk about their learning, know their goals, and create and innovate every day. Is it perfect every day? No. Do we make mistakes, run out of time, and get overwhelmed? Yes. Would we go back to the traditional model after seeing how amazing this process has been for our students and for us? Never! It works. It will work for you, too. One question we get over and over again is about time. How do we find time to do it? Time is always daunting. There are never enough hours in the day. We simply did not let the idea of "not enough time" hold us back. Sometimes we run out of time that day and do not get to every student we intended to work with. Sometimes a certain skill will take longer for a student, and we will need to work with them more to make sure they are able to move on. It happens. But it happens in every classroom regardless of if it is student-led or not. What we do *not* do is waste time. We do not lose time in transition or in lessons that many students do not need because they already understand or are not ready to understand the concept. We don't have twenty students sitting quietly at their desks waiting on the last three students to finish their tests. Have you ever sat through a meeting that was not meaningful to you? How much time did that seem to take? Think about how our students often feel. The bottom line is, we *made* time, and you will too. Will you have to adjust and make changes? Yes. Will some things absolutely not work in your classroom? Yes. Will you be glad you made the change regardless of the growing pains that come along with it? Absolutely!

Remember, this model does take a lot of planning up front. Planning your first unit will take the most amount of time. You need to understand where your students are starting and where they are going. You will need to know how you will check for understanding after each standard or chunk of learning and what the next steps are after students complete their assessments. Give yourself time to plan this. If you teach multiple subjects, we recommend starting this with only one. It allows the students to become acclimated to the new structure while letting you see what works and what doesn't without being too overwhelming. Once you feel comfortable with the one subject, add another. You will see that just beyond the growing pains, there is a classroom that will renew your joy and love for teaching.

It is time to design your first unit. Write down notes as you go through this process.

_____

_____

_____

_____

What are some challenges/struggles/opportunities you faced when planning your first student-led unit?

_____

_____

_____

Now, make this promise to yourself:

I will be proud of my journey to a student-led classroom. I will not try to take on too much at one time, but instead will enjoy the process with my students. I will not be overly critical or allow others to be overly critical. If I need to make changes, I will do so.

Never forget how incredible your profession is. You get to impact our future. It is overwhelming and frustrating and exhausting, but there is nothing more rewarding. Go do amazing things!

Here are a few quotes from our students on our blogs:

"We love the student-led schedule because you can do anything academic you want at any time. You don't feel like you're tied down to your seat all day. It makes you feel more in control. Student-led scheduling IS THE BEST!" (third grade)

"What we like about the student led math class is our independence when working at our own pace. It makes learning more fun and meaningful. When the teacher is teaching you, sometimes you don't pay attention, but with this new student-led model you are forced to really learn it in your own ways. It makes you understand your learning process better." (sixth grade)

"Welcome to the level one hundred student led classroom! We are telling you about what we like about the student-led classroom's student-led schedule. So the first thing is that you get to do what you want to do during the course of the day. The second thing is that this student-led schedule helps us develop things we will always do the rest of our lives no matter what. The last thing we like about the student-led schedule is the coding club. That is where you explore your passion for programming while coding and learning the ways to code." (third grade)

What is your current definition of the student-led classroom?

_____

_____

_____

_____

_____

_____

_____

How has your definition of the student-led classroom changed since beginning the book?

_____

_____

_____

_____

_____

_____

_____

Step 3: *Let Go*

You will probably, like we did, find the first days after your rollout to be a little—for lack of a better term—odd. Here's a true story.

> In the middle school math class, the students were asked to look up the standards they were learning in their math books. On their roadmaps, I had simply left blanks for them to record the standards studied within each module in their math books. We all began on the same module following our rollout—Module 10, to be exact. During those first days, more students than I can count actually asked me where to find Module 10 in their math books! This is minor in the grand scheme of things, but if you refer back to those skills employers are seeking in job candidates, you'll remember that number two on the list was "ability to make decisions and solve problems." My students didn't even have the problem-solving capabilities to consider accessing the table of contents page to help them locate Module 10, or even simpler—not very many of them even considered just flipping through the book, remembering that Module 10 probably

landed somewhere between Modules 9 and 11. Although it sounds like I'm ashamed of my students when they ask us questions like these, it is actually quite the opposite. We, as teachers, are the ones who have trained them to wait for commands. We've always said things like, "Open your books to page 237. Today we will begin Module 10." The traditional school model trains our future, each and every child, to sit quietly and wait to be told what to learn. It takes a few days for the students to shake this.

As your students begin to take ownership in their learning, you will see and hear them growing in beautiful ways. Listen to them; *really* tune in during the first few days after your rollout. Hearing them make discoveries together can help you point out to them and celebrate the *real* learning that is happening behind those discoveries. Here are a couple of stories that offer examples of what we heard when we started, and the connections we helped our students make as a result.

Very soon after the switch in the student-led algebra 1 honors class, a couple of groups of students (this particular class decided to call their self-created groups "companies") began to really take off. These companies were made up of the students who, prior to the switch, would have been daydreaming or otherwise politely disengaging themselves many times during our lessons each day because the pace of "the middle" bored them. Liam and Jake formed one of these companies immediately—the first day after the rollout. They were already great friends and were similar high achievers in math, both conceptually and in the gradebook. In the traditional model, sometimes these students got the eye roll from other students for consistently scoring perfect marks on tests or always having the answers first—before some others had even really started on the problems. Or sometimes students in the class would tell us, "Liam and Jake are eating snacks in the classroom" or "Liam and Jake aren't even doing their warm-up problems," annoyed at the idea that things came so easily to them. I can't define the exact vibe I felt from the students toward these high achievers, but it was a mix of envy, arrogance, and hierarchy, and it wasn't very collaborative or productive on either side. Switching the model changed this vibe completely. Liam and Jake finished the first student-led module before any other group (imagine a collective eye roll from the rest of the class here), but then—something really cool happened. At the beginning of the next class period, as the students (and companies) were setting and sharing their goals for the day, Liam and Jake made an announcement to the class. They told us that they had finished the first module and had taken the assessment and were moving on, but they also (humbly) told us that some vocabulary terms had stumped them on the assessment. They announced that they had created a Quizlet (online flash cards for studying) for everyone in the class to use as they prepared for the assessment on that module—and they'd posted it on the class's online collaboration space to make it accessible to all. A high-achieving, start-up company humbly serving others? We'll take more of that in America, please! This started a trend in the algebra class that created a high-functioning, collaborative group with bonds and connections I'd never experienced before in a classroom—especially a middle school classroom. Let me remind you—these were twelve- and thirteen-year-old students. It was remarkable! This was the type of learning environment you'd expect to find among college students in their specialized areas of study before graduation—students who form groups to study and learn together, students encouraging one another, students bringing new ideas and learning opportunities to their groups of friends. Conversations started changing online, too. Instead of private messages to me for assistance, students became proud to post questions or problems publicly online over the weekend or during the evenings because of the collaboration that was sure to follow. Simply allowing the students to direct their own learning—and to handle it at varying, unique paces—created a foundation of mutual trust and respect among that peer group. I'll always be proud of helping them discover that.

Once you have spent a few days acclimating your students to the student-led learning environment, you will begin to fill that memory book in your mind with small accomplishments, as we continue to do. Seeing Liam and Jake take such delight in serving their classmates (rather than leaving them in their dust) was an accomplishment we will always remember. They found enjoyment in helping others—and found that simply reaching out to their classmates made others more receptive to collaborating with them. They became less isolated and picked up a few valuable communication and social skills; we like to think that they enjoyed testing them out so much that they'll continue to refine them as they mature as students. Although serving others and learning how to create collaborative teams built upon mutual trust aren't exactly *algebra* standards, these *are* lessons/qualities that both parents and CEOs would likely love to see developed in their children and employees.

Shortly after rolling out your new classroom style, keep the next page bookmarked somehow to record the accomplishments you begin to notice. These can be minor (Hey—we are proud that our students now know how to locate pages in a textbook using a table of contents!) or major, like the transformation of Liam, Jake, and the algebra class.

For the Memory Book

Before meeting again with your PLC, list at least three discoveries or accomplishments you've observed that you know are direct results of allowing your students to lead their learning:

_____

_____

_____

_____

_____

_____

Most likely, your students will realize that these transformations are occurring and will let *you* know about them. But they don't always realize the value of the lessons they're learning and how they relate to and impact their futures as capable, durable, and successful adults. You'll find your own ways to help them grasp the magnitude of the learning and growing they'll be doing. You can do this through individual or small-group discussions, or you can bring them up as celebrations during your wrap-up discussions each day or class period.

Cate and Ava

Cate and Ava are the students teachers hope to have on their rosters every August. They are eager and conscientious students who are always looking for ways to help. They are students who could easily be called "teacher's pets." When having whole-group discussions, their hands were the first in the air ready to give the correct answer. It was easy to call on them.

However, amazing students like this can sometimes dominate classroom discussions. The unsure, unconfident students love this, because it means someone else is always willing to answer the questions. So whenever their hands went up, I was torn. I needed to call on others, but Cate and Ava were slightly defeated each time their names were not called.

When we started the student-led model, something I did not expect happened with Cate and Ava. They had trouble talking to others in groups. They enjoyed working in groups but did not help carry the conversations. I asked Cate about it once, and she said that having conversations is different than answering questions. This was a huge wake-up moment for me. In the past, I thought my students and I were having conversations, but that was not true at all. I was in the front of the room talking, and every once in a while, I allowed them to participate by answering a question I gave them. It was my show, and I called on a volunteer from the audience every once in a while.

In the weeks following the rollout of the student-led environment, Cate and Ava bloomed. Although they were extremely nervous at first, they became wonderful group members. They learned to debate issues and truly developed as both leaders and learners. Without the student-led model, these two students easily could have remained great question-answerers and test-takers. Although those skills are highly respected in the traditional classroom, they rarely hold value outside of it.

Maya and Grace

In the sixth-grade student-led math class, a couple of girls named Maya and Grace gave us another memory for the book. Maya and Grace were friends prior to the switch to the student-led classroom. They were conscientious students, rule-followers, and during our whole-group lessons in math class, they were *very* comfortable "self-advocating" when the content wasn't clear. Their frequent interruptions, whether for repetition or clarification, resulted in observable reactions from the other students. Although some students were more polite than others toward

Maya and Grace, it was evident that the majority didn't like having to stop class all the time for them. This took its toll on our classroom environment in a few ways. First, it did offer this particular class lots of repeated and in-depth explanations...this could be seen as a benefit, I suppose. Second, it really slowed us down. We fell behind the other classes in our pacing, and it was really tough to find ways to catch back up. Third, it caused some of the high achievers to simply check out. Bright, inquisitive students, who I knew genuinely loved math, began to appear disengaged and even bored in class. Eventually, the constant questions began causing a collective sigh each time one of them caused us to pause class, and this type of response to a student in a classroom doing exactly what he or she should be doing (questioning) wasn't one I liked seeing. I truly wondered if Maya and Grace would monopolize my time once we switched to the student-led model, holding me captive at their desks, asking me to walk them slowly through each and every lesson, repeating myself as necessary until there wasn't a glimmer of misunderstanding left. But something very different and unexpected happened instead. The day of the rollout, the entire class was fired up. We'd had our classroom discussion, we had seen very positive feedback on the anonymous surveys, and the students were so excited to dive in! The high achievers were suddenly full of life again, smiling, laughing, setting goals and placing friendly bets on who would accomplish the most in the shortest period of time. Maya and Grace were also now free to take their own sweet time (but no one else's) to learn the material in the meticulous, detailed manner they preferred. And both learning styles were suddenly OK. What I didn't expect was that Maya and Grace would actually *keep up* with the previously annoyed high achievers. The first night after the rollout, Maya and Grace went home and—using social media to connect—communicated with a group of about five girls scattered throughout other class periods who were learning the same things. This group of girls took the necessary materials home and worked together online (this is *self-assigned* homework…what?), helping one another as needed, and came to the next class period at the same level as the fast-paced high-achievers. Talk about earning some immediate respect among their previously annoyed peers! Their learning didn't happen miraculously without questions and requests for clarification, though. This group of five girls began meeting in my homeroom class each morning to clear up anything they couldn't all figure out together during class and in the evenings on their group chats. This created yet another memory for our book, because my homeroom class was a standard sixth-grade math class. The first twenty to twenty-five minutes of the day during that homeroom class was "free time," as we waited for all of the students to arrive and for announcements to come on. Maya and Grace and their group of friends turned this time into a morning tutoring session—not only for them, but for the other students in that homeroom class. They started meeting in my room each morning with their list of questions or things they needed help with to keep them on pace with the highest achievers in the class. The struggling math students in that lucky homeroom class were amazed to observe *advanced* math students asking question after question during those morning sessions. (*Advanced* students didn't understand it all and needed help with some things? Who knew!) While previously, the students in Maya and Grace's real math class had become annoyed with their questions, the lower-level math students were hanging on their every word. Watching students model truly advocating for themselves for the sake of deeply understanding content wasn't something they observed frequently in the groups of students they traveled with from class to class. Maya and Grace and their group began teaching my standard homeroom students how to ask good questions and how to ask them confidently without embarrassment. They modeled it for them daily. And my homeroom class began to transform into a place where questions were respected, and the questioners were comfortable because of it.

Step 4: *Connect*

A key to growing as a teacher is to keep company mainly with teachers who uplift you, whose presence inspires you and whose dedication drives you.

—Robert John Meehan

Making connections is key in the student-led model. You will find that connections with your students become much stronger, but having connections outside your classroom is equally important. Let's talk about the importance of some of those connections and how you can strengthen them as you transform your classroom.

Connecting with Other Educators

Do you ever feel like you are surrounded by excuses? Not by your students, but by other educators? When we began this process, we had teachers tell us a million reasons why it would not work in their classrooms. Sometimes they even spoke negatively right in front of us about how we were running our classrooms. It took some time to develop skin thick enough to keep true perspective in those situations. Change can create fear. It can also create excitement and opportunity and inspiration...but not everyone is able to see that right away. That is why it is so important to stay positive with people who share your motivation. We have a group of teachers we trust and depend upon and with whom we are able to share ideas. Before we were coauthors, we were friends who pushed each other to do a little more each day. Our commitment to excellence and to each other is the reason we decided to write this book—as an opportunity for true change—and the reason that we ask you to meet with others once a week. Inspiration is a group effort. We also ask that you document your progress through the Fearless Learners Facebook page, and turn to some "virtual" motivation whenever you need it. Remember, we are here for you as well, and we are truly interested to hear your stories. You can and will create a learning environment that is fun, engaging, and memorable!

Connecting with Administration

We have heard many teachers say, "My principal would never let me do this."

We always answer, "Well, have you asked him/her?" Most of the time, the answer is no. Talking to your principal about how you will implement this model—and why—is important. You are doing this for your students!

Another educator once said that if you want to have more freedom in your teaching, you need to make yourself bulletproof. We have a supportive administration, but our test scores and student growth have increased since we began this model. Our students can talk about their learning and are comfortable sharing what they are working on with anyone who comes into the classroom. It is incredibly difficult to negate that. We have had administrators come into our classroom and say they did not understand the concept. The joy of this is having a student beautifully explain the classroom model and his or her individual journey. It does not get better than that.

Connecting with Parents

Parents. They can be our biggest supporters or our biggest roadblocks. The truth is, they just want what is best for their children, and often the issues occur only due to of lack of understanding or poor communication. Being open and honest about the changes you are making in your classroom is important. We meet with parents and explain the student-led model, and then we make certain promises to them. Those promises usually sound something like this:

- I promise to support your child in his or her unique learning process.

- I promise he/she is learning skills more valuable than the curriculum while also mastering the curriculum fully and completely.
- I promise he/she is not teaching himself/herself.
- I promise to be here if you have any questions/concerns.

Then, we ask that parents commit to supporting the new classroom model. We ask that they encourage their child's leadership skills and allow them to problem solve. We send home the student-led conferences so that the students practice their leadership and communication skills with their parents. We ask questions and value parents' feedback. To us, the parent and teacher are a team. When we conference with a parent, we truly understand the individual needs and learning style of his or her child. We haven't met a parent yet who did not appreciate that.

Connections with Students

It is the connection with students that made us push forward with the student-led model. Our relationships with our students became different, stronger. Now, we should say here that we always had great relationships with our students prior to switching to the student-led model. We always made a point to have interactive classrooms, but too much of that interaction happened from the student's desk. The students who raised their hands were the ones who knew the answers. We missed the ones who were struggling, and we eventually lost those who were bored by material they already knew. Somewhere along the way, we had resorted to teaching to the "middle." Well, that is great for the middle, but what about everyone else? This is where it became important to teach like a parent. What if your child was on the higher or lower end of this educational spectrum? Would you still be OK if your child's teacher was reaching *most* of the students?

We make a point to give our students a say in all aspects of the classroom. We share our pacing guides and are open about what we can change and what we can't. We survey students and parents, asking their opinions on everything from the student-led model to our teaching styles, inviting input on any changes they would make. We ask them periodically if they want to continue the model. This is always a collaborative yes, but be careful to respond appropriately when students do say no. Give careful attention to working through the why in those situations. Often we find that the student has never been given responsibility or freedom before and it is scary, or that it requires them to do, think, and learn more. Those are the students who end up benefiting the most.

We develop a relationship of trust with our students. In elementary school, we make a sign that says "I promise…" where student and teacher write down commitments to one another. The one that comes up time and again is "I promise to work hard every day and never give up." We set meeting norms and remind students (and ourselves) to make sure we follow them when we meet in small groups or one-on-one. When the students know we trust and value them, they take that responsibility seriously. Think about your favorite teachers in school. Weren't you motivated to work hard for them? Didn't you want to make them (and yourself) proud? Now, think of a teacher (or employer) who you do not feel valued you. Was the motivation to please that person still there?

It is important to remember that this classroom environment is not built overnight. It takes classroom meetings and encouraging students. It takes supporting students while they become comfortable in the new model. But here is the payoff—you really get to talk to them. As soon as you see a student struggling, you can help. In this model, feedback becomes almost immediate. Due to the fact that students test at their own pace, there is no stack of papers to grade at the end of the day. If you have one or two students taking a test, you can grade the tests the moment they're completed, and you get to provide immediate and personalized feedback the same day. However, you will find that grades improve exponentially when students are assessment-ready. This leads to higher confidence, which equals more motivation, which leads to teacher bliss!

Connecting through Social Media

We have a confession—not long ago, we never would have written this section. We thought our social media life and our teaching life should be completely separate. Teachers go to great lengths to learn the privacy settings of their social media account of choice. We make sure no one can find us. We use aliases or some altered version of our names. We do this to protect our private lives. We, as well as many other teachers, had trouble finding the value of social media as it related to our classroom. We were inspired to give Twitter a try for several reasons. We knew other well-known educators in our county were using it, and we were curious to have a peek inside their classrooms. We also knew there had to be educators outside of our area that we would be able to learn from. According to Brett Baker, an account executive at Twitter.com, out of the half a billion tweets that post every day, 4.2 million are related to education (Edsurge, 2014). Talk about connection! At our school, we had some trailblazers willing to figure out Twitter, and they helped us out along the way. We created accounts, and our school created a hashtag. We began to see value in sharing ideas, but we were takers only. We loved it when our coworkers posted something innovative or got excited about their students' work, but we rarely posted anything ourselves. It seemed pretentious, as if we were bragging about something that we were still trying to figure out. We had completely missed the point of connecting through social media. If you wait to share it until it is perfect, you never will. People want to see the process. Teachers (well, most teachers) want to cheer one another on. An environment needs to be created where teachers encourage one another, share ideas, and celebrate successes. You can start that environment! Share your ideas. Be an open book. Follow us on Twitter at @christysutton27 and @kristinwestberr, as well as @studentledclass. We will follow you back and help you connect to other powerful educators just like yourself.

You have hopefully also joined our Facebook group, Fearless Learners. Here you can create posts, share ideas, and collaborate with other amazing educators.

Step 5: *Fail*

Success is not final, failure is not fatal. **It is the courage to continue that counts.**

—Winston Churchill

Of all the content in this book, we consider ourselves to be special experts in the art of failing. We've done lots of it. From mishandling questions from parents wondering why we "don't teach anymore" in the student-led model (communication fail), to the gut-wrenching realization two weeks before the standardized test that some of our students weren't on track to even be introduced to the last grade-level standards in the year's curriculum, much less master them all (planning fail)—we have *experience* with failing. It happened to us, and it may happen to you. What we also have, though, is passionate dedication—a deep-rooted belief that we are committed to providing the very best type of education we can to our students as their teachers. We've felt the almost tangible energy the student-led model has brought back to our classrooms, and we never want to go back after experiencing something so powerful and fulfilling. Our students have come alive with learning—they're delighted to find out what curious, capable people they truly are in a classroom where anything is possible and failure is welcomed, presenting opportunities to press on, grow, and make new discoveries. So as we experience failure, as teachers who are challenging the status quo and trying something different for our students, *we do not give up*. Instead, we graciously forgive ourselves. We objectively and productively reflect on our mistakes. Then we make positive adjustments and carry on. And last, but not least, we usually repeat the entire process lots of times in a continual effort to improve. We continue to fail, reflect, grow, and improve, but once again—and most importantly—*we never give up*. We hope your experiences with your students in the student-led classroom will inspire and instill the same growth-minded perseverance when you experience setbacks.

There's this really simple plan for losing weight that we all know works better than any pill, any diet, any personal training program, any *anything*: simply managing the calorie balance. As long as our calorie intake doesn't exceed our calorie burn, we'll lose weight. It's a very simple mathematical concept. The same simplicity applies to how we have learned to handle mistakes and failures using the student-led classroom model. As long as our passion exceeds the sting of our failures, we are able to carry on confidently, growing better and better with each and every

~~failure~~ *opportunity* to provide an even richer educational experience for each and every child in our classrooms.

Here are two suggestions for you to keep in mind before we vulnerably and unashamedly begin sharing with you how we've grown through our failures:

1. Don't ever give up. Make adjustments, but *press on*. Keep the passion for what you are doing for your students just a little greater than the sting of your failures. Tweak things as you go, and persevere. And if you get discouraged along the way, don't worry—your students will offer daily reminders of why what you're doing is so wonderfully important, should your passion need a little kick in the rear.

2. Don't take the setbacks too seriously. Laugh! Remember the promises you made to yourself before you began this transformational journey, and let those minor setbacks help you to pause, reflect, grow, and shape you and your classroom into something even better. The children are watching and learning from your responses to failure.

Now—we would like to share the following stories with you so that you can (1) learn from our failures simply by reading about them, and (2) hopefully avoid the growing pains of actually making these specific mistakes during your own classroom transformations.

~~Fail~~ Lesson #1: Thinking we wouldn't fail. (What were we thinking?)

We both agree that our biggest mistake going into this was thinking we'd get it mostly right on our first shot. Probably a lot like you, we became inspired to change the model; we dreamed up the richest educational environments we could imagine for our students; we carefully planned out our transformations; we actually followed through and saw our plans into reality; and then—things just did not go perfectly. As you read through the following stories of our specific pitfalls and roadblocks, know that they were both personal and painful for us as we experienced them. But really considering our mistakes and writing to you about them here has helped us to realize the gift each failure actually was and still is to us. Each and every one of them stopped us in our tracks and demanded that we carefully consider and revise pieces of the student-led model that truly needed changing. We now know that our greatest "failure" has been the assumption that eventually we would *perfect* the model, be done with failure and change, and write to you about how to manage your own classroom transformations completely flawlessly. We are thankful for and humbled by the discovery that the perfect model does not—and never will—exist. We have since adopted a healthier philosophy: we are eager to welcome failures, and we even seek them out, as they are the gifts that keep us growing.

So we ask that you read this mission statement and make this promise to yourself. Refer to it as needed. As you go through implementing the model, you will experience failure.

"I accept that there's no perfect classroom model; I embrace it! I welcome failures and appreciate them for the gifts they are—opportunities to grow. I will, despite any setbacks, remain ruthless in my attempt to provide every one of my students with the educational opportunity the student-led classroom provides."

*Signature*_____

*Date*_____

~~Fail~~ Lesson #2: Liam and Jake

Does this dynamic duo sound familiar? They're the two friends from the algebra class who formed a "company" and moved with lightning-quick speed through complicated algebra concepts, much to the amazement (and the occasional eye rolling) of their other classmates. Who knew this team would present my first classroom fail?

When I first rolled out the new model and watched with anticipation to see where the kids would take it, I never imagined that any student or group of students would go home after a class on Friday and spend no less than ten hours together over the weekend finishing a module I had planned would take most of the students about *two weeks* to finish! Nor did I dare to dream that the same group of students would go home after the very next class period and Skype/work together for another ten hours or so in the evenings to finish the second (and last) student-led module that I had planned for them. After finishing that second module in record time, Liam and Jake asked me for the next module—which I hadn't made yet. Writing this, I still feel the shame I felt the day they asked me...

We told you this transformation would be amazing, but in fairness, we've got to tell you how much time it takes to adequately plan it all out in the beginning. You can't plan for the middle anymore. You've got to either plan well ahead of the middle or have a plan in place for students who could master your grade-level content tomorrow.

~~Fail~~ Lesson #3: Need Help? Get in Line!

During the first days following the rollout, we noticed a few things right away. First, we were active in this new model—really, really active! We had anticipated circulating the classroom and facilitating the learning, but neither of us expected the numbers on our step-counters to *double* under the new model. We were in high demand. Students were engaged, excited, and learning, but that meant that they had questions (lots of them) and that they wanted to share things (everything) with us! We heard our names being called all over the room, all the time. We amused ourselves with new memory games during each class period as we challenged ourselves to keep ordered, mental lists of the students who needed our attention.

It wasn't working. Too many students needed our attention, and it was taking too long to get to them.

After a few exhausted afternoons spent wondering why we were so tired and what could be done differently, we discovered part of the solution ourselves, while our students actually contributed the other part.

The roadmaps used to guide the students were originally designed with lots of teacher check-ins in place. How else would we know if the students were truly doing the assignments correctly and learning unless we checked their work ourselves? But it just wasn't feasible. We had to be everywhere at once, checking over all types of activities, since the kids were all working on different things. Other students just needed our help or a little mini-lesson on something that needed clarification. But sometimes the "line" for help and checking was so long that some students just gave up and moved on. This was one of those failures that caused us to pause, reflect, and make positive adjustments. First, we took a hard look at the learning activities we were offering the students in each module, and we redesigned them so that more of them were self-checking. Students could, we learned, be trusted to check some of their own work. They enjoyed it, even, and we had more time to spend conferencing with individuals and small groups as originally intended.

The second solution to this problem was a combined contribution from both a student and a fellow teacher—the Expert Board. During a class period where the line for help was getting pretty long, one of our students started a list on the board. She just called it "Help" and listed her name first; she encouraged her other friends waiting for the teacher to do the same. This helped us remember to visit each student or group on the list, and it also alleviated the students' need for hand raising or leaving their group or activity to come find the teacher. Then it evolved a little bit. The students started writing what they needed help with beside their names on the list; other students took notice and began offering *their* help. As students helped each other, they crossed their own names off of the list. Remember the advice in "Connect" to get out and visit other classrooms as much as you can? It turns out Christy's classroom had an even more elegant solution already in place. One quick visit to her room revealed a student-created and managed expert board, where any student who felt comfortable enough with certain content or a learning activity added his or her name to the expert board so that others would know who to turn to for guidance in those areas. The students loved listing themselves as experts, and they enjoyed the opportunity to collaborate with their classmates as they worked through problems together. Just like that, the happy hum of the productive, engaging, student-led classroom returned. Problem solved.

~~Fail~~ Lesson #4: Two Weeks Left

In the curriculum in our county, there is a very cut-and-dried, crystal-clear list of lessons the students must learn prior to *the test*. As teachers in the student-led model, we had two ways to track the students' progress through the lessons on our end. One was the giant visual in the back of the room, which the students used to celebrate their success (they moved a personalized clothespin up a ribbon each time they mastered a module); the other was the gaps in our grade book. If we wanted to see which students were lagging behind, we could spot names on the clothespins at the bottom of the ribbon and encourage those students. In the gradebook, progress was even easier to view. Every assignment, project, assessment, or activity was graded immediately upon completion. This is one of the best things about the student-led model actually—the immediate feedback the model provides to the students. Recording the grades immediately helped us notice gaps in the gradebook. It gave us a clear picture of those students who had fallen behind and needed guidance, direction, or even a quick conference with Mom and Dad (if they were too far behind). There were students in sixth grade, though, who fell behind and truly didn't have an easy-to-solve laziness issue. They were working hard day in and day out— struggling because they had been left behind with so many gaps in their knowledge, which widened further with each passing year in school. Imagine trying to find the surface area of a multisided object with fractional dimensions when you still have to use your fingers or skip-count to multiply whole numbers. Ideally, these students should have been working on third-grade concepts—we should have met them exactly where they were first left behind and worked on filling gaps. But there's this test...so we compromised. We let these students continue to work through the sixth-grade material, but we let them do it at a pace that allowed for us to spend a great deal of time helping them in their individual gap areas (remember Jacob's discovery?). This helped them. We got e-mails like this one from the parents of these students:

I want to thank you for being such an outstanding math teacher. Iris loves math. She has never loved ANYTHING SCHOOL RELATED before! I am not exaggerating I promise. She truly has not enjoyed school until this year. I know you were a big part of that, and I cannot express into words how much I appreciate it!

Thanks from a very grateful mom!

We loved seeing these students enjoying school again, feeling pride and accomplishment, and gaining confidence in their abilities. And then, suddenly, it was two weeks before *the test*, and that group of students was too far behind to finish the sixth-grade curriculum before its arrival. Planning fail. We panicked, and then we improvised. We designed a series of whole-group lessons that would cover all of the content in time; we interrupted the student-led model for about half of each class period so that all of the students in our classes would have at least heard about all of the material on the test when they had to take it. This was heartbreaking for us, because once again we saw those needy students glaze over when we stood in front of the classroom talking about standard deviation and variation in data sets. They still needed to work on their times tables. We saw boredom on the faces of high-achievers again. There isn't a perfect solution here. The problem is really big. For these students, we had to go back and restructure. What did we miss? Were they really making the most use of their time? Did we involve the parents enough to help at home? We temporarily fixed the problem by providing a lot of individual support and many less than desirable whole-group lessons. However, we made a plan going forward to give overviews of the approximate time in which standards should be mastered. Parents were provided this information as well. Then, when students were not ready by that time, we as teachers—along with parents at home—were able to give much more support so we did not run out of time before the standardized test.

~~Fail~~ Lesson #5: ESE—"This isn't working for us."

One of our student-led classrooms had a large ESE population, and two additional teachers assisted during that class. After the rollout, we were particularly proud of the learning gains we noticed in that class (Jacob was in that class), and the parents of students in that class couldn't tell us enough how their students' attitudes toward school had changed. A couple of students from that class actually joined an after-school Math Counts team! The tests we used to track growth over the course of the year showed enormous growth in this particular class. We delighted in all of it—these types of successes kept our level of passion greater than the sting of our failures and made us believe in what we were doing for the kids. One day during lunch, though, one of the ESE teachers approached us with a problem. She had noticed three students in our class who were not giving their best efforts. She felt that these students were flying under the radar and using the model to cover for their lack of motivation or willingness to work. She was right. Until she pointed this out, the two ESE teachers in the room would circulate, just like the regular classroom teacher, helping and teaching students at their individual levels as needed. Once we discovered that there were a few capable yet unmotivated students using the cover of the model to pretend the material was too difficult for them, we had to pause, reflect, and make some positive changes. Two things helped solve this problem: the must-do lists and positioning the ESE/support teachers differently. The must-do lists were created to help the students keep their learning on track. As educated adults, both of us live by our calendars—we are goal-, date-, and deadline-driven, and our students are no different. The "have-to-by" lists provide the students with an overview of tasks and goals to accomplish within a certain timeframe. These lists helped make our crafty "fly under the radar" students' progress very visible to us again. The other solution to this problem was to create a semi-permanent small group, facilitated by the ESE teacher. Once these students had been identified, we had them work together in a group with a dedicated teacher who helped them make continuous progress. The students missed the freedom of the student-led group and became motivated to prove they were capable of managing their own must-do lists. Win-win.

We have failed. We will continue to fail. You might too. The difference is whether we crumble or grow from each setback, and that is a simple choice we can all make.

Take a look at how you currently handle failure. Where do you see yourself on this spectrum? I tend to…

|--|

| Blame myself when things in the classroom go wrong. Experience a high degree of guilt. Go hard on myself and feel ashamed of my mistakes. | Recognize that failures present opportunities to improve. Easily look past blaming myself or others for failures and proactively search for positive adjustments I can make. |

Think about your own classroom transformation. What would you consider to be failures during the process to date? Give those failures "titles" and list them below. Then, beside those failures, list the responses and, if possible, the solutions that a teacher on the right end of the spectrum would facilitate:

Titled Failures   Positive Responses

_____   _____

_____   _____

_____   _____

_____   _____

_____   _____

From failure to growth. From challenge to elegant solution. It's a beautiful cycle that can propel us to unparalleled successes or leave us miserably complaining in the teacher's lounge or at the lunch table. And it's as simple as choosing a deliberately positive response.

How we choose to handle our various setbacks really proves how successful we will be in any endeavor, and it's no different with our efforts to transform the traditional classroom model. Thankfully it starts with a choice we are all capable of making. Each time you hit a roadblock, face a challenge, feel the sting of a failure in some regard, look back at the spectrum above and deliberately make the choice to compassionately guide yourself to the response on the right.

Step 6: *Celebrate*

We struggled when we began to write this step. Celebrating is hard. Who critiques themselves more than a teacher? No one. Contrary to some beliefs, we are not in teaching for the money, the summers off, or the low job stress (we could not even write that without laughing). We are in it for the ability to make a difference in the life of each student. We get to impact the future. It really is amazing! Yet, because of the tremendous importance and demands of our job, we never feel like we are doing quite enough. Paperwork, e-mails, and documenting data are rarely completed to the level we hope for. We spend hours on lesson plans each week—trying to plan the elusive perfect lesson. We take our jobs seriously, and when we do decide to leave our laptop at school or not think about the classroom for an entire weekend, we feel guilty. Then we go on Pinterest and see the perfect little classrooms with all their organization and color, and we think of the stacks of papers that cover our desks and that we have not changed our bulletin boards for four months. There is little time for celebration within that guilt, criticizing, and constant comparing. We started with one simple idea—Start—and we end with this one—Stop. Stop downplaying yourself and your contribution to education. It is time to celebrate!

It is easy to become an island while teaching. It is much like the old question, "If a tree falls in the forest and no one is around to see it, does it make a sound?" For us, this would translate to "If something flawless happens in the classroom and no other adults see it, does it hold value?" Not only does it hold value, but it should be celebrated! Go tell the teacher next door, tweet it out, or e-mail us. We will celebrate with you! Be excited about your classroom, and you will find that excitement is contagious. Your students will feel it and so will other teachers. You get what you give, and if you give positivity, you will attract it.

We also recommend being open about your classroom being a work in progress, but never be self-deprecating. Great teachers are always evolving. As they know better, they do better. They are constantly looking for the next step. You are helping to reform education. Having a student-led classroom is something many students will never get to experience…but yours will. Be proud.

There were two events that happened recently that made me realize the importance of what I am doing in my classroom. I was at a wedding for a fellow teacher, so (as you can imagine) there were many teachers attending. One teacher started asking about what I taught and about the classroom setup in elementary school (she taught

163

high school). I began telling her about my classroom and how my students moved at their own paces, assessed when they were ready, and even made their own daily schedules. She just shook her head and talked about how amazing that had to be for the students. She had never seen another teacher do it, but as we talked, she realized how she had pieces of the student-led model in her own classroom. She committed then to talk to her students about choice the next week. She did and now has a student-led model that works for her. She e-mailed me recently and talked about how she wished she would have made those changes sooner. I think about how if I had not celebrated my success with her, she might never have made them.

The second event happened outside the world of education. My husband and I were on a weekend getaway (we have three children—this never happens!) and stayed at the most wonderful bed-and-breakfast. We were talking to another couple, and the wife mentioned that they restored old houses. I am a huge fan of restoration, and we connected. She told me that people who enjoy making old things new tend to do this in all areas of life. She asked what I did for a living, and I told her I was a teacher. She asked how I made my teaching new. I told her about the student-led model, and she said I was not just making my classroom new but changing the idea of education. It turned out that she was a former college professor. She said that students often came in without the skills needed to find success in the real world. She actually thanked me at the end of our conversation, and it felt undeserved. It is just my little classroom with the blended ideas of so many other educators who had been brave enough to celebrate with me. But it does matter. Every day matters.

These stories are important because they show the ripple effect of celebrating. You will allow yourself the privilege of being proud of your classroom and your students while also inspiring others to further benefit *their* students. Not everyone will want to celebrate with you. Some people will make excuses or downplay the amazingness that is your classroom. That is OK, because there are many people who will get excited alongside you. They will celebrate with you within success and within failure. Failing truly does mean you are *trying,* which automatically puts you ahead of many people, right?

Is it difficult for you to share ideas/progress/success? Why or why not?

_____

_____

_____

_____

_____

_____

_____

The student-led model is not easy. It is not a simple fix to all of our educational problems. However, allowing students to gain the skills, not just the knowledge, they will need as adults will make a difference in our future.

What is something you can celebrate about your classroom right now?

_____

_____

_____

_____

_____

As we become more comfortable with celebrating, we encourage the same for our students. They talk freely about how proud they are of their accomplishments when something works, as well as their struggles when something doesn't. We are not competing with one another. We are all on the same team, and one success is a moment to celebrate and gain inspiration and perspective from. It takes some time to develop this environment, but it is so worth it. Here is an example:

We have morning and afternoon meetings where all the students sit together and we discuss any important issues for that day. These last about fifteen to twenty minutes each. I, as the teacher, make any announcements necessary, but the rest is student-led. One student is chosen at random to lead the discussion each, day and they often ask questions like "What are you working on today?" or "Any failures from yesterday that you are going to turn to successes today?" The students answer and get to share any cool projects or ideas they are having. This is one of the most valuable times in the classroom, because not only are students celebrating, but they are also inspiring one another.

One day, a student started talking about completing an innovation project, but wanted to incorporate math and science skills. The students brainstormed together for a moment and found that his interest was cooking. (Keep in mind, this is all led by them. I am a participant in the conversation, but I do not direct it.) They quickly connected cooking to fractions, measurement, and chemical/physical change. The student decided then to have cooking classes at his house. Another student mentioned he had been working to raise money for a non-profit organization dedicated to helping childhood cancer research. So the cooking classes also became an opportunity to donate money to this organization. Several students participated, and money was raised for the Children's Cancer Society. Now, think about this for a moment and look at the connection within the classroom. A student created the opportunity to be a teacher, the students participating in the class got to learn a new skill, and a wonderful organization was helped...all because we celebrated.

Another example of this occurred in our afternoon meeting. A student was excited because she had mastered a math skill she had been working on for quite a while. She talked about how confusing it was and that she thought she would never master it, but that in group, it had just made sense. The other students clapped and gave a lot of praise. Then another student raised her hand. This student is shy and incredibly anxious about not doing well. She wants to hide in the shadows, so the student-led model, although out of her comfort zone, has been good for her. As the student-moderator called on her, she told her how she had been working on the same skill, but it had never made sense before. She asked to schedule a help session with the student who had mastered the skill the following day. They quickly discovered a time that worked for both of them. I had met with both of those students many times for this particular math skill. For one, it was in that group that it finally made sense. For the other, it was her peer that best explained it in a way that she connected to. This might not have happened if not for celebration.

Somewhere along the way, we began to tie celebrating to bragging and placed it in a negative context. Yet, all successful people share what makes them successful. As teachers, we hold our accomplishments close to us and worry about anyone finding out. Part of this is the competitive environment that has been created in many schools. The other part is our own fear. We are scared of being judged or hurting others' feelings. Complaining is the new popular way of dealing with the problems. Those negative environments are exhausting, though. They drain you and make it difficult to enjoy the process. Remember what inspiration feels like each time you are in these situations. Always be the positive one. Celebrate! Be *fearless*! It can change people's direction and perspective.

We have an open-door policy in our classrooms. When people ask when they can come in, we say anytime. Are there bad times to come in? Of course, but we want them to have a true look into our classrooms on any given day. We have had fellow teachers, administrators, district leaders, and other innovators from different counties or companies come in, and we planned nothing outside of our regular day. The joy of the student-led classroom is that we do not have to create anything or be puppeteers. The students are on personal journeys in their learning, and there is not a whole-group lesson or a show we can put on that is greater than that. We also visit as many classrooms as we can. We sit down with other teachers to share ideas. These collaboration sessions are "where the magic happens." They rejuvenate us and help keep us moving in the right direction. We read professional books and follow inspiring educators on Twitter. We take in as much information as we can and then find what works for us.

So, while you are out celebrating with the world, remember to also do so within your own classroom. When a student perseveres and finds success in a difficult skill, we celebrate. When a student notices a mistake, even if they don't know how to fix it (yet), we celebrate. When they tell us about winning a sports competition or meeting a personal goal, we celebrate. We often stop the class to celebrate. We used to wait until the end of the day or class period, but we soon realized how important these bits of inspiration are throughout the day. Students, like adults, love to be recognized. When we learn to recognize them for the skills that are important—leadership, perseverance, kindness—and not grades, these celebrations become all the more meaningful.

Now, we do not want to give the impression that we eat, sleep, and breathe school. One of the things we are learning to celebrate is balance. We are both mothers to young children and have our own crazy schedules outside of school. Since implementing the student-led model, we actually have more balance. As we said, there is a lot of work up front. You have to plan where your students are going. After that, you are meeting and helping and watching in amazement. There are no hours and hours trying to create some perfect lesson. You don't stand at the copier every morning. We really only copy assessments, unless it is something we are using for a small group or an individual student. You no longer spend each night grading. Papers are handed in only a few at a time and can usually be graded the same day. The work we do outside of school has become more meaningful and long term. We say balance is a great thing to celebrate.

Keep in mind that you do not celebrate perfection; you celebrate *progress*. You can create an environment that you are proud of and uplifted by...one in which you are positioned to encourage others. This is your moment for change. You are walking toward a classroom that both you and your students are excited to enter every day. Find something in each day of that process to celebrate! Celebrate your students, and always take the time to celebrate *you*!

Thank you for taking this journey with us. As you move forward with the student-led model, remember to encourage your students and yourself to be fearless. There are amazing things to come!

This PLC is created to help you on your journey to a student-led classroom. It is organized to include six weekly meetings. Although we've created an outline for each meeting, the goal is to have meaningful, thought-provoking, forward-thinking discussions with your peers.

Enjoy the process. Hopefully, you will continue to meet long after your six weeks are completed and you have successfully implemented a student-led classroom.

Week 1

Date: _____

Participants:_____
_____
_____

The purpose of the meeting this week is to begin talking about the student-led classroom and how you will begin working toward your goals. You will also need to establish meeting norms to make sure these PLC meetings are productive and remain a positive, motivating environment.

Meeting Norms Established by Your Group:

_____
_____
_____
_____
_____
_____

Goals for Week 1 PLC:

_____Create a definition for the student-led classroom.

_____Determine your overall goals for the student-led classroom.

_____Discuss your strengths and those of your fellow teachers.

_____Address worries/concerns about the student-led model.

_____Decide which subject you are starting with and what the students will use to monitor their progress, such as maps, scales, etc. You can find examples of these on our Facebook page.

_____ List immediate changes you need to make in your classroom in order to make the student-led model successful.

Discussion questions for Week 1 PLC:

1. Share your definition of the student-led classroom from the introduction.
2. What are your goals in creating this classroom model?
3. Name three strengths you have as a teacher that will benefit others in the PLC? What strengths do you have that will benefit your students?
4. Discuss your worries/concerns about the student-led model.
5. Will you be starting with one subject/class period? If so, which one? If you are not sure, make this decision with the support of your PLC team. Are you and your group members starting with the same subjects?
6. How will your students use scales/success criteria maps/roadmaps to guide their learning? Again, if you are not sure, make this decision together.
7. What are some immediate changes you need to make to your classroom in order to begin transitioning to the student-led model?

Decide:

How will you and your PLC partners communicate with one another: email, One Note (this is a great option, especially if you have several people in your group), social media/Edmodo, etc.? This needs to be something you are committed to checking on a daily basis to ask/answer questions, share ideas, and celebrate successes and failures.

Your next PLC date: _____

Action Steps (please complete this before the Week 2 PLC):

- Complete the Classroom Discussion Guide on page 61.
- Have your students complete the Exit Slip on page 62.
- Tally responses from question one on Exit Slip (page 62)
- Review question 2 on the survey and discuss any concerns individually with students.
- Come up with your own survey questions on page 76.

Notes:

_____
_____
_____
_____
_____
_____
_____
_____
_____
_____
_____
_____
_____

Week 2

Date: _____

Participants:_____

_____

_____

Goals for Week 2 PLC:

_____ Discuss classroom discussion and Exit Slip results.

_____Continue developing scales/roadmaps/success criteria plans.

_____Discuss how students will prove their learning (formative assessments, checkpoints, mini-assessments).

_____Finalize survey questions (page 76).

Discussion Questions for Week 2 PLC:

1. Go over results of your classroom discussion. Any surprises? Did anything stand out?
2. Discuss your Exit Slip results.
3. Were your results similar to those of your group members? Why do you think this is true?
4. Discuss scales/success criteria maps/roadmaps and how your students will be navigating through their learning. If you do not know yet, this is an excellent topic to brainstorm on and create a plan together.
5. How will you set up the process of students leading their own learning? You talked about scales/maps last week. This week talk about checkpoints—how will you give

mini-checks to make sure students are learning before their assessments. Remember, these can be conversations as well as written or computer-based assessments.

6. Share the survey questions you created on page 76.

Decide:

Decide where in the curriculum you are starting. If starting at the beginning of the year, start with the first set of standards for your subject. If starting midyear, start with your current or next set of standards.

Your next PLC date: _____

Action Steps (please complete before the Week 3 PLC):

- Make one change in your classroom that promotes the student-led environment.
- Begin creating the necessary support for students to go through the first unit in your student-led classroom. This includes the scale/map, assessments, checkpoints, and any activities or resources you will make available. You will have two weeks to complete this, but remember, we expect this to take somewhere between six and eight hours, so start right away.

Notes:

_____
_____
_____
_____

Week 3

Date: _____

Participants:_____
_____
_____

Goals for Week 3 PLC:

____Share progress in creating first unit activities.

____Create steps in rolling out the student-led environment in your classroom.

Discussion Questions for Week 3 PLC:

1. Discuss successes/failures in creating your first unit's activities.
2. What are your expectations for this first week of implementing the student-led environment with your students? What are you excited about? What are you not looking forward to?

Decide:

What are your steps to roll out the student-led environment in your classroom? Share these and offer feedback to one another.

Your next PLC date: _____

Action Steps (please complete before the Week 4 PLC):

• Complete your unit plans.

Notes:

Week 4

Date: _____

Participants:_____
_____
_____

Goals for the Week 4 PLC:

____Share completed unit plans.

____Finalize plans for the first unit based on feedback from PLC team members.

Discussion Questions for Week 4 PLC:

1. Share your completed unit plans.
2. Discuss any reservations you have with beginning the student-led classroom.

Your next PLC date: _____

Action Steps (please complete before the Week 5 PLC):

- It begins...you will start the process of implementing the student-led classroom with your students. Explain to students how they will travel through their learning. Talk about your checkpoints and how they will be able to determine when they are assessment ready. ** Explain their options for working toward mastery of a standard.

- After you have answered the students' questions, begin the student-led process. For the first day or so, you may just want to walk around and check on the students. This is the time that it is very important to set those expectations for the student-led environment.
- Write down observations this week to share with your PLC group.
- **We do have a request here—give the students options, but do not make these activities too structured. For example, if you have a student working on equivalent fractions, we have websites such as IXL, Study Island, Kahn Academy, or Discovery Education they can work on. We also have games and activities we (or others) have created, which we make available. We have small group meetings where we offer lessons to help with the concept. Textbooks can also act as a resource. We promote experts in the classroom (i.e., students who have shown mastery in that skill and can help other people). These are not center rotations—it is not "Spend fifteen minutes here and switch." That is still teacher-directed. We want the students to have choice. Many times, our students do not pick any of the options we have given them. They meet and have conversations where they create problems, or our experts will make games for others. The goal is that they are learning—they are moving forward with their knowledge in the skill.

Notes:

_____

_____

_____

_____

_____

_____

_____

_____

_____

_____

_____

_____

Week 5 PLC

Date: _____

Participants:_____
_____
_____
_____

You probably have a lot to discuss this week! We hope the first week went well and that you are well on your way to an effective student-led model. We also understand there were probably a couple of bumps in the road. Sharing these in your PLC will benefit the group going forward.

Goals for Week 5 PLC:

_____Discuss your first week implementing the model.

_____Decide what adjustments need to be made in order to support your vision for the student-led model.

Discussion Questions for Week 5 PLC:

1. How do you feel after implementing the student-led model?
2. What were some of the reactions of your students?
3. What worked well? What did not?
4. What are changes you need to make moving forward?

Your next PLC date: _____

Action Steps: (please complete prior to Week 6 PLC):

- Adjustments! Have a whole-group discussion with your students about what they felt worked well and what did not in the first week of the student-led model.
- Begin making these adjustments to iron out any problems that occurred last week.
- Start preparing the next unit's activities. You may have students ready to move forward, and you'll need to plan ahead to be ready when they are.

Notes:

_____
_____
_____
_____
_____
_____
_____
_____
_____
_____
_____
_____
_____
_____
_____
_____
_____
_____
_____
_____
_____
_____
_____
_____

Week 6

Date: _____

Participants:_____

_____

_____

This is the last official PLC meeting, although we hope you continue these weekly meetings. Classrooms are forever a work in progress.

Goals for the Week 6 PLC:

_____Discuss your survey results.

_____Brainstorm ideas for giving students a voice through newsletters or blogs.

_____Discuss how you can encourage students' passions through Innovation Time projects.

_____Decide on must-do lists.

_____Decide on changes needed moving forward.

_____Make a date and time to visit another PLC member's classroom.

_____Decide if you will continue to meet as a group to discuss progress.

Discussion Questions for the Week 6 PLC:

1. Talk about your survey results. How are your students feeling about the new model?
2. Discuss setting up a classroom blog or newsletter.

3. Have you started Innovation Time (for students to explore their individual interests) in your classroom? If not, how can this be implemented?
4. Discuss the idea of having a weekly must-do or deadline date for units. Would this help students still move at their own pace while also making sure they complete the standards necessary for quarter/semester/year?
5. How did the changes/updates that you made improve your classroom model?
6. Are there any areas you still do not feel comfortable with? Are there adjustments you can continue to make in order to improve these?
7. How are you determining who you meet with in small group? Are you getting to all students? Why or why not?
8. How will you handle students who are not progressing through the standards and are falling far behind in the pacing guide? Do you have any students this is currently happening with? Is it behavioral, or are they genuinely struggling with the material? How can you ensure these students master the material but continue to work at a steady pace?
9. Make a plan to visit one another's classrooms. There is no replacement for seeing the student-led model in action to gain ideas and inspiration.

Meeting with: _____

   Date and Time: _____

Action Steps following the Week 6 PLC:

- Continue to make adjustments.
- Meet with those students who are beginning to fall behind.
- Continue to work toward completing future units.

Notes:

be fearless

References

Covey, Steven R. 2008. *The Leader In Me: How Schools and Parents around the World Are Inspiring Greatness, One Child at a Time.* New York, NY: Free Press.

Edmodo. 2008. "Edmodo." July 6, 2016. www.edmodo.com

EdSurge. 2014. "Twitter Exec Reports that Educators Dominate the Twitter-sphere." Katrina Stevens. June 28, 2016. https://www.edsurge.com/news/2014-04-30-twitter-exec-reports-that-educators-dominate-the-twitter-sphere

Forbes. 2014. "The 10 Skills Employers Most Want In 2015 Graduates." Susan Adams. May 20, 2016. http://www.forbes.com/sites/susanadams/2014/11/12/the-10-skills-employers-most-want-in-2015-graduates/#3635eba219f6

Kahn, Salman. 2012. *The One World Schoolhouse: Education Reimagined.* New York, NY: Twelve.

Merriam-Webster Online. 2016. "Design." October 13, 2016. http://www.merriam-webster.com/dictionary/design

TEDTalks. 2006. "Ken Robinson—Do Schools Kill Creativity?" Sir Ken Robinson.June 8, 2016. https://www.ted.com/talks/ken_robinson_says_schools_kill_creativity

Wong, Harry K. 2009. *The First Days of School: How to be an Effective Teacher.* Mountain View, CA: Harry K. Wong Publications.

CPSIA information can be obtained
at www.ICGtesting.com
Printed in the USA
LVOW13s2347191216
518023LV00007B/848/P